Completely transform the atmosphere of your learning environment with these simple but powerful educational techniques.

"[This] is a guide to turning every teacher into an artist of the spirit and is an important contribution to the bookshelf of any teacher profoundly interested in the world within us and not only in the world outside of us."

—from the Foreword

The time has come for a new direction in education. The goal is no longer to teach good class, to convey information or even to have the students enjoy the learning. Soulful Education is about enabling another—child, adolescent, adult—to discover how to become his or her best self through learning.

In this inspiring call to a radically different kind of teaching, you will gain:

- Skills to help you connect the material being taught with your students' souls, to support your students in envisioning and reaching their potential.
- Tools to help you best use your position of influence, whether you are a parent, educator, professional, lay leader, rabbi—anyone whose role is to guide, encourage, mold and motivate.
- Tips for using the wisdom of the Jewish tradition as a springboard to help students get in touch with their truest selves and step boldly forward on a path of lifelong growth.

Through his personal journey, and the methodology and authentic questions he has developed, Aryeh Ben David offers us a path to unleash the creative force in our students, our sacred texts and, perhaps most importantly, ourselves."

—**Rabbi Marc Baker**, Head of School, Gann Academy

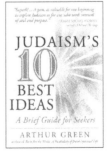

Rabbi Aryeh Ben David, a world-renowned educator, is committed to plucking the soul strings of teachers and students alike in order to transform how we learn and grow. He is the founder of Ayeka: Center for Soulful Jewish Education, which trains educators of all denominations, campus professionals, and staff of middle and high schools how to teach Jewish subjects with more soulfulness, personal meaning and impact on life. Formerly he was a senior faculty member and director of spiritual education at the Pardes Institute in Jerusalem. He has been the keynote speaker for national conferences of Reform, Conservative and Orthodox rabbis, and has served as the educational consultant for Hillel International for three years.

Dr. Erica Brown is an educator and author who consults for non-profits and currently serves as the community scholar for The Jewish Center in Manhattan. The recipient of a Covenant Award for her work in education, she is author of *Inspired Jewish Leadership: Practical Approaches to Building Strong Communities*, among other books.

"Zeroes in on *the* most pressing issue within the field of Jewish education today: How can we get young people to truly connect with Torah in a deep, genuine and transformative way?... An essential text for anyone seeking to become 'soulful' and impactful educators."

—**Rabbi Ari Segal**, Head of School, Shalhevet High School

Also Available

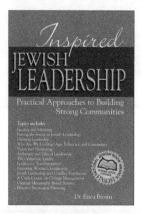

Inspired Jewish Leadership
Practical Approaches to Building Strong Communities
By Dr. Erica Brown
Takes a broad look at positions of leadership in the modern Jewish community and the qualities and skills you need in order to succeed in these positions.
6 x 9, 256 pp, HC, 978-1-58023-361-3

Relational Judaism
Using the Power of Relationships to Transform the Jewish Community
By Dr. Ron Wolfson
Guides Jewish lay leaders, professionals and community members in transforming institutions into inspiring communities.
6 x 9, 288 pp, HC, 978-1-58023-666-9

Dr. Ron Wolfson
Author of The Spirituality of Welcoming: How to Transform Your Congregation into a Sacred Community

For People of All Faiths, All Backgrounds
JEWISH LIGHTS Publishing
an imprint of Turner Publishing

BECOMING A SOULFUL EDUCATOR

How to Bring Jewish Learning
from Our Minds,
to Our Hearts,
to Our Souls—
and into Our Lives

ARYEH BEN DAVID

FOREWORD BY DR. ERICA BROWN

For People of All Faiths, All Backgrounds

JEWISH LIGHTS Publishing
Woodstock, Vermont

Becoming a Soulful Educator:
How to Bring Jewish Learning from Our Minds, to Our Hearts, to Our Souls—and into Our Lives

2016 Quality Paperback Edition, First Printing
© 2016 by Aryeh Ben David
Foreword © 2016 by Erica Brown

Library of Congress Cataloging-in-Publication Data
Names: Ben David, Aryeh, author.
Title: Becoming a soulful educator : how to bring Jewish learning from our
    minds, to our hearts, to our souls-and into our lives / Aryeh Ben David ;
    foreword by Dr. Erica Brown.
Description: Woodstock, VT : Jewish Lights Publishing, [2016] | Includes
    bibliographical references.
Identifiers: LCCN 2016018702| ISBN 9781580238731 (pbk.) | ISBN 9781580238786
    (ebook)
Subjects: LCSH: Judaism—Study and teaching.
Classification: LCC BM70 .B36 2016 | DDC 296.6/8—dc23
LC record available at https://lccn.loc.gov/2016018702

10 9 8 7 6 5 4 3 2 1

Manufactured in the United States of America
Cover Design: Jenny Buono
Cover Art: © KieferPix/Shutterstock.com
Interior Design: Thor Goodrich

For People of All Faiths, All Backgrounds
Published by Jewish Lights Publishing
A Division of LongHill Partners, Inc.
Sunset Farm Offices, Route 4, P.O. Box 237
Woodstock, VT 05091
Tel: (802) 457-4000   Fax: (802) 457-4004
www.jewishlights.com

This book is dedicated to the soulful educators who changed my life:

Rav Abraham Isaac HaCohen Kook
"In the education of an individual, and so too with the education of the collective, the nation and all of humanity, we need to pay special attention to spiritual unity."

Parker J. Palmer
"The transformation of teaching begins in the transformation of the heart of the teacher."

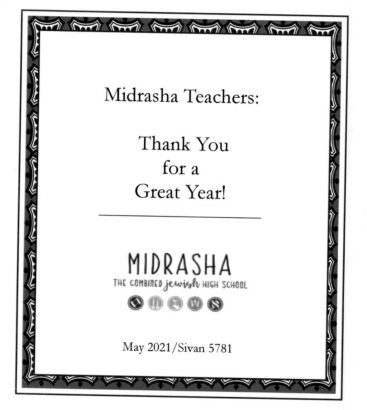

Midrasha Teachers:

Thank You
for a
Great Year!

MIDRASHA
THE COMBINED *jewish* HIGH SCHOOL

May 2021/Sivan 5781

Contents

Foreword

Who would *not* want to become a soulful educator?

We all want to reach people in a deep, immersive way when it comes to the areas of life that matter most. That's why we picked education. But in between classes, many of us worry—I certainly do—that what we are teaching is not entering the hearts and minds of our students. Perhaps it's just intellectual meandering, dry and arid, at times even brittle.

Becoming a Soulful Educator is a guide to turning every teacher into an artist of the spirit and is an important contribution to the bookshelf of any teacher profoundly interested in the world within us and not only in the world outside of us.

"A single day is enough to make us a little larger or, another time, a little smaller." The artist Paul Klee wrote these words, and they describe well what many artists and educators feel as they approach a new canvas or a new day. Sometimes all goes well, and we have moments of professional triumph. We are creative. We are strong. We are able to communicate what moves us with passion and clarity. We feel enlarged by the mission of our work and inspired. We are able to unfold a small sliver of holiness and transcendence. On those days, we cannot imagine doing anything else for a living. At times like this, teaching is not a job. It's not even a career. It's a calling.

But on other days, we find ourselves relating more to Klee's sense of smallness. Humbled by knowledge and learning or by the nagging voice inside that says, "Just give up. This isn't for you. No one is paying attention. No one is changing as a result of anything you're teaching." The black cloud parks above us all day, and we wonder why we didn't go to law school or become investment bankers.

Virtually every master educator I know cares about transformative change and sees himself or herself as an educational change agent. Unless you can make people uncomfortable enough to question basic assumptions about self and other but loved enough to take risks, it's hard to help any student make any visible difference. And we need to so that we can push the black clouds away and bask in the radiance of the good days.

Aryeh Ben David is a master educator who knows a great deal about change—in his own life and in the lives of his students—and now hopefully in the lives of teachers who want to become great at what they do by reaching deep inside and bringing that inside out. You won't become a soulful educator just by reading the book. But if you move from the text to life and internalize its lessons, you will be a different kind of educator.

Dr. Erica Brown

Who Is This Book For?

This book is for educators—for anyone working in formal or informal education, whether for children or seniors or anyone in between.

We ask you to take a step back from your teaching, to take a long hard look at the impact you are making—versus the impact you want to make, the impact you became a teacher to make. And if you, like so many of us, find a disconnect between the two, we offer suggestions to help you grow as an educator, to become a soulful educator.

This book came from my own experience, my own personal journey. For my first fifteen years as a teacher, I was a pretty good educator, but not a soulful educator. I taught, my students learned, and we all benefited from the experience.

But my teaching was not making the life impact that I wanted my students to experience. Truth be told, my teaching wasn't making the impact on myself that I wanted it to either. There was something lacking, something unfulfilling about the entire process. My students would have benefited—and I would surely have been a better teacher—if I had had a book like this to guide me at the beginning of my career.

A soulful educator is someone who wants to enable students, whether children, adolescents, or adults, to discover their better selves through learning. We all have souls, we all have infinite potential, and we are all on a never-ending journey to become the best we can be. We're not there yet—actually, we will never be.

So how do we get there? Or more correctly, how do we get nearer there? And as teachers, how do we help our students get there?

Soulful Education, taught by soulful educators, can be one piece of the journey. Soulful educators are the people in our lives who help us reach our potential. We all have had teachers like this at one point or another:

that special advisor we remember with so much gratitude, the homeroom or drama teacher who saw us for who we could be, the math or football coach who believed in our deepest capabilities. Unfortunately, most of us can point to only a handful of these teachers in our decades of formal education. But what a difference they made. And where did these precious people learn the skills they used to reach us? For the most part, through intuition and trial and error.

The name of our organization that promotes Soulful Education is Ayeka. *Ayeka* ("Where are you?") is the first question of the Torah and echoes eternally. In the Garden of Eden, Adam couldn't answer the question and hid from God. Our better self is always hiding from us, waiting to be discovered. We chose the name also because it was a question. We do not come to provide answers but to help people hide a bit less from themselves, to discover their better self which is always yearning to be known.

So the questions Soulful Education asks is this: the skills that enable educators to reach their students, to connect the material being taught with their students' souls, to support their students in envisioning and reaching their potential—can these skills be taught? Are there tools that we can offer to parents, educators, professionals, lay leaders, rabbis—to the myriad people who are positioned to guide, encourage, mold, and motivate—to help them best use their positions of influence? And as Jewish soulful educators, is there a way that we can use the great wisdom of our tradition as it was intended, as a springboard that helps people get in touch with their truest selves and to step boldly forward on a path of lifelong growth?

I am absolutely convinced that the answer is yes. Over the past ten years, Ayeka and I have been experimenting with simple but powerful educational techniques that have completely transformed the atmosphere of scores of classrooms across the United States and in Israel. In parallel, they have transformed my own approach to the educational enterprise, returning to me the sense of mission and fulfillment that brought me to teaching in the first place. I invite you to join us in this journey and to be part of the revolution, the age-old and ever-new practice of Soulful Education.

Acknowledgments

The Talmud states, "The air of Israel makes one wise" (*Baba Batra* 168b). I have been given the privilege to live in the Land of Israel and breathe its air. Though I have no claims to be wise, there is no question that this book was conceived, born, and grew through the gift of the air of Israel. I humbly and gratefully acknowledge the generations of ancestors who, while being scattered throughout the world, remembered Israel and Jerusalem. The prayers of countless individuals of the past are present between the words and lines on every page of this book.

After two thousand years of wandering, the Jewish People returned to their home. This historic miracle has given me and others hope. It is my dream and vision that Ayeka and this book will continue this chain of hope, pushing us all to take steps to make this world a bit closer to being in the image of God. I believe there is no greater gift one can give than hope. We have been blessed to receive it; Ayeka aspires to continue bestowing this gift.

Anyone who has ever engaged in a new project knows that success comes only after many bumps in the road, and Ayeka has been no exception. This is one of the reasons we believe a hidden hand from above has been silently guiding our endeavors.

Words cannot express my appreciation and love for the Ayeka team. Yehoshua Looks's experienced wisdom has guided our start-up to new heights. Leora Niderberg's calming proficiency and artistic creativity infuse all that we do. Ilana Sinclair has worked tirelessly to bring Ayeka's message to the larger world.

We are grateful for the kindred spirits close by who have shared their time, energy, and insights. The Ayeka Israel Board—including Mick Weinstein, Lois Liebowitz, Corey Beinhaker, Dasee Berkowitz, Clare Goldwater, and Tzvi Schostak—"heard us to speech." The chairperson of our board, friend and soul mate David Kahn, has walked every step of our journey, shining the light needed for our next steps.

I could not have taken the first steps of Soulful Education without the wisdom and insights of my colleague and friend Rabbi Zvi Hirschfield. Mali Brofsky brings joy, dedication, and spiritual anchoring to all of Ayeka's pursuits. It is our honor to have them on the Ayeka faculty.

I am indebted to the kindred spirits who always gave supportive voices—Yoni Barnhard, Stuart Meyers, Mark Banschick, Steve Zerobnick, Sheryl Adler, Pearl Mattenson, and Nina Bruder. You offered me the deep friendship, inspiration, and confidence to sit and write.

Two role models mentored me during the very first years of my teaching career, and their words of wisdom and encouragement have never left me. Thank you, Bob Bleiweiss and Dr. Robert Barnhard.

The graceful and wise editing touch of Noga Fisher adorns every page.

Parker J. Palmer's luminous wisdom and experience have served as a model for all of Ayeka's striving for authenticity and its educational break-throughs. The brilliance and *menschlichkeit* of his educational vision—the Center for Courage & Renewal—has been a model for Ayeka's path and growth.

The Shalhevet High School of Los Angeles and the Kohelet Yeshiva High School of Philadelphia placed their trust in us. We are grateful to Rabbis Ari Segal, Noam Weissman, and Ari Schwarzberg, and Rabbi Gil and Melissa Perl for their educational vision and dedication to the professional growth of their staffs.

We are very thankful for the steadfast backing of Julie Frank, May Shee-han, and the Sharna & Irvin Frank Foundation. None of Ayeka's achievements would have been possible without their generous support and vision.

Without the vision and professionalism of Stuart M. Matlins, Emily Wichland, and the Jewish Lights staff, this book would still be a manu-script sitting in my desk drawer.

It is impossible to thank enough the kindred spirits in the world of Jewish education who are tirelessly toiling in the fields of the classroom, campuses, and synagogues and whose dedication nurtures and ensures the brightness of our future.

My wife and co-traveler, Sandra, our kids and their spouses, Shachar and Zev, Ma'ayan and Elishav, Amichai, Yaniv, Ra'aya, and Lilach, have blessed me with their unwavering support and love and have enabled the dream of Ayeka to become a reality. They have gracefully endured being the laboratory for Abba's Soulful Education experiments throughout their entire lives and have become soulful educators for the next generation—our grandkids, their communities, and the Jewish People as a whole.

With gratitude,
Aryeh Ben David
Director of Ayeka

Introduction

Writing this book has not been an easy task. With every statement I make that calls for a change in the educational status quo, I see legions of dedicated, talented, and experienced teachers standing before me, bristling at my temerity to question their goals and accomplishments. And yet, I can hold myself back no longer.

A friend advised me to imagine myself standing on a rooftop, screaming out my truth as boldly and loudly as I could. For me, a person who is timid by nature and has hardly ever yelled, this advice was daunting, unnerving, scary, overwhelming … but here goes. This is what I want to shout from the rooftop of every synagogue, day school, yeshiva, and Jewish community center:

> "Wake up! Wake up! It's not about 'learning,' it's about 'meaning'! When we don't connect with the hearts, souls, and lives of our students, we are just wasting our time."

Whew. There, I said it.

Imagine this scenario: It's the last day of class. Two students approach.

One says, "Thanks so much. I loved your class. I learned so much. I loved the discussions and was really stimulated by your thinking. By the way, the class didn't actually affect me so much—I just didn't connect to the subject personally. But I learned a ton. Thanks!"

The other says, "You know, I wasn't the greatest student in your class. I daydreamed and didn't understand everything. But something in the class touched and changed me. I feel like it's become a part of me; it helped me figure out who I am and what I want to be. I'm sorry that I was such a lousy student, but I want to thank you from the bottom of my heart."

Obviously, what we want is for students to learn the information we teach *and* to be affected by it, to know and to grow. But if you could choose just one or the other, which would you choose?

This book is written for educators who would choose the second scenario.

That wouldn't have been me at the beginning of my career. For twenty years, I taught in Jewish settings with a preference for the first scenario. Teaching Jewish sources was my profession and my calling, and people told me that I was good at it. But at some point, I began to realize that the goal was not just teaching a good class and that the mark of a good class was not just students with a good understanding of the material. I came to see that the moment of truth—the true test of my teaching—occurred after the class was over, that it was measured in the way that students approached their lives over time. The goal of teaching was not teaching, it was living.

In other words, I had been putting the wrong destination into my educational GPS. Although it took time, I came to understand that I needed to revise my route. Pushing knowledge into the minds of my students had value as a worthy milestone toward reaching the final destination. But it was not the final destination.

This is a book about bringing another dimension into the classroom, about how we, as teachers, can bring our souls and those of our students into play.

My Crisis as a Teacher

I always dreamed of becoming a teacher, and my dream came true at a young age. In my thirties, I had the great privilege of teaching adults at three wonderful institutions: Pardes Institute of Jewish Studies and Livnot U'Lehibanot in Jerusalem, and as a consultant for Hillel International. In my heart of hearts, I thought I would spend my whole life in those classrooms. Five years of teaching became ten, and ten became fifteen. I was fulfilled and happy; I loved my students and often felt their affection in return.

But then in my fifteenth year of teaching, things began to change for me. Nothing dramatic occurred; there was thankfully no external event, no life-threatening disease or serious accident. But something began to shift inside me. Increasingly, I started to sense that I was entering into a crisis.

It began as a small unsettling feeling. The teaching was going well: students were learning and motivated, I was popular, my superiors were delighted, and I already had my contract for the next year. But something was flat, wrong, lacking.

Over time, I began to put words to this feeling. The mind-focused style of learning that I had pursued for so many years was simply not enough. The mission that I had been taught to pursue was to achieve intellectual mastery of a broad range of timeless Jewish sources and to pass this on to my students. I was pretty good at this, and it was fulfilling, up to a point. But it was falling short.

By the middle of the year, what had begun as a small, nagging feeling had grown to become a constant uneasiness. By the end of the year, I felt as if I were being strangled by an invisible force. Something had broken. After fifteen years of what was considered by many to be successful teaching, I simply couldn't continue teaching in the same way. A relentless inner voice was begging me to acknowledge what I always should have known: *true Jewish wisdom is much, much, much more than information.*

So when I turned fifty, I did something crazy. I left a wonderful position with job security, prestige, and a decent livelihood to pursue the question that wouldn't let me sleep: how can Jewish education become transformative? My own introduction to Jewish wisdom, at a relatively late age, had transformed my life. Why was it that it wasn't always transformative and life-altering for my students, who were learning so well?

I realized that something was being left out of the learning process, something important. I knew that I could not continue in the same way as before, but it actually took me three years to work up the courage to make a change. With six kids and no clear vision of where my vision would lead, I was terrified.

But I did not turn back. I began experimenting with educational approaches and techniques aimed at making a tighter connection between our wonderful Jewish sources and the deep inner lives of my students. With every step, I became more convinced of the soundness of this direction, more assured that this is what Jewish education needs. As I grew more and more passionate, I actually became more and more practical, and a clear approach that could be adopted by conventional teachers became more and more evident. At some point several years ago, I actually couldn't have turned back if I had wanted to.

I gave this new approach a name: Soulful Education. And I spoke about the need for Soulful Education with every educator I met.

For the first five years, my earnestness was usually met with glazed eyes and whispers, "What happened to Aryeh? He used to be a serious guy, a good teacher. It seems that he's flaked out." But over time, I began to see interest. People started listening, acknowledging that something was missing from their own teaching. Deep within, they knew I was right: Jewish education needed to be—deserved to be—much, much more than just the transmission of knowledge.

Now, ten years later, it seems that the whole Jewish world has woken up to this point of view. Jewish educators in every setting and denomination are feeling an urgent need to open hearts, to touch souls, to make student interaction with Jewish knowledge as personal, meaningful, and life-changing as possible.

We are obviously not starting from zero in the pursuit of this goal. Jewish teachers have always been motivated by the deepest goals and are astoundingly dedicated to their students. And teachers of this generation are better educated and have studied more pedagogy than any generation in history. Plenty of students *are* personally affected by the material they are taught, but one thing is clear: too often, the emphasis of Jewish schooling on the transmission of quantities of information leaves a majority of students feeling bored and disconnected.

- A growing wave of principals, educators, and rabbis are alarmed at the disconnect. Their students aren't bringing the Jewish wisdom that they feel so passionate about into their lives; their hearts just aren't in it. Their learning remains dispirited and passionless.
- A group of women who have been learning together seriously for twenty years approach me and ask, "We're looking for a deeper connection to the sources, and we don't know how to get there. Where do we start?"
- A principal calls and says, "Our students are learning well. But they don't seem to really connect with it. What can we do?"
- Students graduating from a prestigious high school say to me, "We learned a ton. But our teachers were more interested in the material than in us. We wished they had taught less and listened more. Can that happen?"

My personal crisis as an educator seems to have been a weathervane, a warning that a crisis was brewing in Jewish education. Awareness of the need for Soulful Education has intensified and will continue to grow. Why did this happen?

The Old GPS of Jewish Education: Knowledge and Continuity

All education, consciously or subconsciously, has an agenda; all education systems prioritize the values that they want to pass on the most.[1] In Jewish history, it is clear that different values and qualities have been emphasized in different eras and by different religious leaders:

- In nineteenth-century Western Europe, Rabbi Samson Raphael Hirsch focused on obedience to the law and punctilious religious observance. A century earlier, in Eastern Europe, the Ba'al Shem Tov spun tales for souls yearning to find a direct channel to God.
- In mid-twentieth-century America, Rabbi Abraham Joshua Heschel wrote about educating for "wonder and radical amazement." At the same time, Rav Abraham Isaac Kook educated for *menschlichkeit* (high moral standards).
- In late twentieth-century America, the dynasty of Rabbi Joseph B. Soloveitchik stressed rigorous intellectual challenge and discipline.

It is fair to say that the primary goal of Jewish education, at least for the past fifty years, has been Jewish continuity—the simple preservation of the Jewish People. In practice, this resulted in a focus on "education for the sake of identification." Fueled by the losses of the Holocaust and the fear of assimilation, there was an understandable focus on preservation through familiarity with Jewish history, tradition, and philosophy.

Therefore, Jewish education focused on the transmission of information, calling for the learning of Jewish texts, the memorization of historical facts, and the familiarization with the Hebrew language and Jewish liturgy. In some settings, the desire to master content became an obsession; there are lots and lots of books on the Jewish bookshelf, and the goal of Jewish education was to get through as many of them as possible.

Please don't think that I am belittling the value of Jewish learning or minimizing the accomplishments of those who have become masters of the Jewish wisdom passed down from sage to sage through the millennia. As a people who lived for centuries without a land or a government, and with such limited control of the circumstances of our lives, it is nothing short of miraculous that Judaism has survived and thrived, and these sources were the anchor that made survival possible. However, the knowledge culture that evolved, when divorced from personal connection, misses the mark and is now alienating rather than attracting many of our best and brightest.

This is different from before. For hundreds of years, the *beit midrash* (house of study) was the center of the Jewish community, and its focus was exclusively on understanding the holy books. Those who knew more received more honor, and the most respected figure of all was the *talmid chacham*, the scholar with the deepest mastery of Jewish texts. Great masters offered deep insights into the hearts of man. But most students—and their teachers—were satisfied with a breadth of learning that didn't pierce the soul. Similar to academic settings, in which it is unthinkable to use the phrases "I think" or "I connect to," Jewish learning was an impersonal endeavor. Intellectual rigor, objectivity, and emotional distance were valued.

This was certainly my own experience in the *batei midrash* where I learned. My study partner, Daniel, and I had an almost fanatical desire to cover as much material as possible. My rabbi once told me that his definition of a *talmid chacham* was someone who has mastered five tractates of Talmud with their primary commentaries. To him, the consummate learning achievement was defined in terms of quantity. Is it any wonder that it never occurred to us to ask questions such as:

- Does this line or phrase resonate with me?
- How do I connect to this commentary?
- How can I bring the concepts of this book into my own life?

I began my day in the *beit midrash* at 4:15 a.m. and studied until my eyes could no longer focus. One year, Daniel and I learned the tractate of *Kiddushin*, which covers the laws of marriage. We fell in love with this tractate and learned it again and again. Not once did we ask each other, "How could this material affect our marriages?" Not once.

This level of awareness simply wasn't on our radar screen. Even if some-one had dared to raise the question, we probably would have scoffed. We had a single, focused ambition: to understand and master the material. There was no time for feelings.

The desire to learn more and more occupied all of our time and emo-tional energy. This precluded ever taking the time to stop, process, and connect personally with the texts we were studying. How could we slow down when we had barely opened a fraction of the holy, important, and scholarly books on the shelves?

My mind was fully present in the *beit midrash*. We heard the beautiful, resonant voices of the authors of our holy texts: Hillel, Shammai, Rabbi Akiva, Maimonides, the Ba'al Shem Tov, and many others. But I did not know how to let these voices create a similar resonance inside me. My own voice was silent.

At the time, this did not bother me. In fact, I was not even aware of the disconnect. I was absorbing greater and greater quantities of information, so my learning was successful. Today, however, this cerebral approach is resonating less with students. Why? There has been an explosion in information access. Virtually all of Judaism's wisdom sources have been translated into accessible languages, and the Internet offers nearly limit-less access to all subjects. Classes are offered online in almost every Jewish topic and are available 24/7.

I recently attended a conference in which a world-renowned personality gave a talk about the Chofetz Chaim, a central scholar in modern Jewish history. He spent minute after agonizing minute recounting factual details of the great man's life. After just thirty minutes, more than half of the audi-ence had left—including me, I am embarrassed to say.

Why did we leave? None of us had the patience to listen to informa-tion that's easier to access at our leisure on a smartphone. In a lecture, we look for more: for insight, connection, perspective, relevance. In fact, the classroom has all but lost its relevance as a venue for transmission of knowledge exclusively.

So what is the classroom the place for? What can we do that is valuable in the classroom? What can we give students in a classroom setting that they can't acquire for themselves, that in fact they can't find anywhere else?

The New GPS of Jewish Learning: "Becoming"— A Call to My Future Self

Jewish learning is about the future. It is not supposed to be about the past. However, we must learn from the past to improve our judgment, to help us grow, to equip us for the future.

The ultimate purpose of learning Jewish wisdom is to put me in direct contact with the voice of my soul, to equip me to play my role in rebuilding paradise, to help me create a better *me* and a better future. Looked at in this way, the goal of Jewish learning is future oriented, focused on "becoming" rather than on the past, even if the way we get there involves learning about thousands of years of people, history, and thought.

This new goal of Jewish learning is, in fact, very old. It was mentioned almost two thousand years ago in the Talmud:

> Rabbi Tarfon and the Elders were once reclining in the upper story of Nitza's house in Lod, when this question was raised before them: "Is study greater, or practice?"
>
> Rabbi Tarfon answered, saying, "Practice is greater."
>
> Rabbi Akiva answered, saying, "Study is greater."
>
> Then all the Elders answered and said, "Study is greater, for it leads to action." (Talmud, *Kiddushin* 40b)

A great Jewish thinker, the Maharal (Rabbi Judah Loew ben Bezalel, 1520–1609), expands, "For study to be great, it needs to be the impetus that naturally and directly leads the learner to action."[2] Study needs to impel students to renew and improve their lives. For study to be great, the knowledge acquired needs to be transformative, a springboard for personal growth and change.

However, in our time, Jewish education often falls short of this goal, becoming a purely intellectual experience with the study itself as the end goal.

As a student, I once learned in a yeshiva where the goal was to stump the rabbi with the hardest or most complicated question. When I was training to be a teacher, the dean of my school told us that the end goal of our work would be to teach students how to become independent in learning medieval commentaries.

Whether as students or teachers-in-training, we were not encouraged—in fact, we were almost discouraged—from seeking personal *insight* from the texts that we were learning. Study was not expected to lead to action. There was no effort to search for personal meaning, no attempt to filter the content we acquired into our lives. The scope of education was limited strictly to the pages in the books.

I used to think that this was just the approach of the schools where I learned. However, I have discovered that this narrow vision is the rule rather than the exception. I have asked countless educators, "When you teach, what is the most important moment for your students?" Usually I receive answers like these:

- "The 'aha' moment, when you can see the eyes of the students light up."
- "The class discussion—when it is active and dynamic, and everyone is into it!"
- "The end of the class when I give over my new understanding of the subject. It changes the way the students relate to the topic with a whoosh—and this is so exciting!"

From the Soulful Education perspective, the answer is different:

- The most important moment for the student happens *after the class is over*. The goal of teaching is not the class experience—it's life itself. When a class is effective, the students take the wisdom we study and use it to make a difference in their lives. It isn't about *learning*; it's about *becoming*.

This is identical to the conclusion that the Talmud's elders came to so long ago. But over time, this wisdom was lost. The focus of learning shifted to quantity over impact, with the after-class effect assumed to be the student's personal matter—nice if it happened, not necessary if it didn't; an afterthought.

I once asked an experienced and popular Talmud teacher, "How do you help your students integrate their learning and bring it into their lives?" He replied, "It happens automatically. The students naturally incorporate this kind of learning into their daily lives. We don't need to take time away from the learning itself to belabor what will occur by itself."

I am not so sure. When I was a student, I certainly never "naturally incorporated" my learning into my life. Was I the only one?

Then, when I became a teacher, I found my own goals to be the performance-oriented measurements that so many of my colleagues continue to pursue today. I was intoxicated with the vibrancy of the classroom, loving it when everyone spoke at once, arguing passionately about the subject. The class was captivating, stimulating. I wasn't boring! I felt validated as a teacher. I was satisfied with the outcome: I had touched their minds and stimulated their thinking. And the students themselves were satisfied: they had now learned the subject matter well and even enjoyed the process.

But the most important piece, the leading-to-action piece, was missing. The excitement and passion of the students often ended when the class was finished. Neither the students nor I were even aware of this lacuna. We had so shrunk our definition of "education" that life and action seemed irrelevant. Learning was all about the intellect: questioning, arguing, discussing, and then moving on to the next page.

I'm all for thinking, questioning, arguing, and having great class discussions. But none of these will necessarily bring the learning into the lives of our students. None will naturally fulfill the Talmud's advice: "Study is greater, for it leads to action."

I can learn about love and not become a loving person. I can learn about jealousy and remain jealous. I can learn about Shabbat while never knowing how to make Shabbes. I can learn about the Jewish People without feeling connected.

For students to bring learning into their lives, they need it to touch them in a very deep place. The material they learn—the texts that they are exposed to—must penetrate into their core beings, into their souls. They need to internalize the ideas in order to feel a need to bring them into their lives.

For this to happen, teachers must devote time and focus to the after-class experience, to the ongoing effect of the learning. For most teachers, this requires a huge paradigm shift, a reshaping of their pedagogic goals. They must set out from the moment they begin planning the class to touch the souls of their students so deeply that the learning becomes part of their life story *after the class is over*.

Now, to be sure, I am not saying that every class must be life changing. But I am stating, unequivocally, that the big-picture teaching goal should be to impact lives for the long term, well after the class is over. This focus should be the underlying current, the soul of Jewish teaching. I can promise you, from my own experience, just starting with this goal will make a huge change in what you teach and how you teach it.

I believe that this approach represents a new mind-set for most teachers. Most have never considered their role in shaping their students' lives and certainly accept only limited responsibility for such a weighty influence.

But this is exactly what I believe is needed in Jewish education. The goal of the enterprise must be redirected from simple continuity to transformative change. We must move from the "knowledge for survival" paradigm to "know to grow."

Asking the New Questions

You might ask, "Okay, just how do you expect me to do that?"

This different educational approach raises new questions:

- How exactly do I go about evoking the souls of my students?
- How does the heart learn, in contrast to the mind?
- How can I enable my students to authentically and personally integrate Jewish knowledge into their lives?

And most importantly:

- Is there a system I can use to accomplish these goals, one that is not dependent on the personality or charisma of the teacher?
- Is there a system that will work for me and other teachers, for all types of subjects and students, in all types of settings?

For a shift toward Soulful Education to succeed, teachers need a new system of education—a new pedagogy—that will enable our students to become touched and transformed by the information that they learn.

The goal of this book is to present such a system, appropriate for all teachers and all subjects, which will enable our students to grow and be transformed by our teaching. It has been refined through years of experience in real classrooms of all sorts, throughout the United States and

Israel, with a broad range of teachers. It is mindful of the fact that today's world is a world of choice and that tomorrow's students will continue learning from Jewish wisdom only if it is made personally meaningful and inspiring.

Part 1

Laying the Foundation for Soulful Education

To create the Soulful Education paradigm, we first need to address four essential questions:

What does it mean to be a soulful person?

What does it mean to be a soulful teacher?

How do I create soulful space?

How do I love *all* my students?

We'll examine these questions in part 1 and will follow this up in part 2 by answering how we can bring soulfulness into everything we teach.

What Does It Mean to Be a Soulful Person?

The Voice of the Soul

I don't really *choose* to become a soulful person, just like I don't *choose* to become a physical person. As a person born with a body, I am, by default, a physical being. I can choose to take care of my body, to listen and attend to the needs of my physical self—or not.

So too I was born with a soul. The beginning of the Torah introduces me to myself: "God formed Man from the dust of the ground, and breathed into him the breath of life; and Man became a living soul" (Genesis 2:7). As with my bodily needs, I can choose to take care of my soul, to listen and attend to the needs of my spiritual self—or not.

I know what my body wants. It conveys its needs and desires loud and clear, telling me directly, "I want to eat, I need to sleep, I want to be satisfied, now!" What about my soul? Does it also have a voice?

Rav Abraham Isaac Kook writes that our souls are always speaking to us.[1] In his language, the soul is always "whispering, singing, or praying." The soul is not inert, not just a lump of spirituality that somehow dwells within me. The soul is not dormant, waking up only when I walk on the beach at sunset, see a double rainbow, or have a spiritually rousing experience. The soul is always alive and, like my body, has its own voice. What does my soul say? What is it whispering, singing, and praying to me?

The answer lies in the beginning of the Torah. God creates Adam and Eve and places them in the Garden of Eden. God then commands them to refrain from eating from the Tree of Knowledge of Good and Evil. We know the story: the snake, Eve eating from the tree, giving the fruit to Adam, God kicking them out of paradise, God forbidding them to return.

What is not always understood is that Adam and Eve's banishment from the Garden of Eden was also part of the divine plan. It was inevitable that they, or their descendants, would eventually eat from the tree. According to tradition, Adam and Eve were in the Garden of Eden for about twenty minutes before calamity struck. That's about as long as we can resist temptation.

The Kabbalah makes it clear that God planned for Adam and Eve to be kicked out of the Garden of Eden.[2] It was all a setup.

I once worked as a waiter in a restaurant with a gigantic kitchen. One entire wall of the kitchen was lined with drawers, and each drawer had a label. Salt. Pepper. Nutmeg. Sponges. Ladles. Hundreds of labels. One drawer was labeled "Do not open." It didn't take me twenty minutes to open that drawer. I'm not sure if it even took twenty seconds. It was irresistible. There could not have been a greater incentive for me to open it than to make it off-limits.

As soon as God told Adam, "You may eat from every tree in the garden except that one, the Tree of Knowledge of Good and Evil," his fate was sealed. As surely as the sun rises in the east, one day Adam and Eve would eat from the forbidden tree, and then they would be exiled from the Garden of Eden. Why would God play such a mean trick?

It is tragic but true that we are hard-wired to yearn for something after we have lost it. We cannot yearn for an abstract idea that we have never experienced. Only by tasting something and then losing it do we feel the pain of loss and then create a passionate desire to taste it again. Adam and Eve bequeathed to us the yearning for paradise.

Jewish wisdom revisits this paradigm of brokenness and loss again and again, always to create a sense of mourning at what has been lost and a yearning to re-create:

- The Midrash says that an angel visits the baby in utero and teaches it all of Torah, then touches the baby's lips during the birth, causing the baby to forget all of its learning. This loss creates the yearning to learn and "remember" Torah (Talmud, *Niddah* 30b).
- Moses brought the first tablets down from Mount Sinai, only to shatter them (Talmud, *Baba Batra* 14a).
- Maimonides writes that King Solomon built the First Temple in Jerusalem with the awareness that it would be destroyed.[3]

• The Kabbalah teaches us that God created the world through the breaking of the holy vessels of light.[4]

We yearn for things we have lost, and this yearning is the DNA of our souls. The more precious the value of the object lost, the greater our yearning. God placed Adam and Eve in paradise, even if only for twenty minutes, to provoke the yearning for a paradise lost. Although they can never return, they can build a new paradise on this earth. In fact, the rest of the Bible is a blueprint for the re-creation of paradise in our world.

Just as each person has a unique face, fingerprints, voice, taste buds, and body, so too each person has a unique soul designed with the specific characteristics needed to accomplish a specific repair in our world.

So what does our soul whisper to us? Each soul enters this world with a unique role to play in the rebuilding of paradise. Just as each person has a unique face, fingerprints, voice, taste buds, and body, so too each person has a unique soul designed with the specific characteristics needed to accomplish a specific repair in our world. I did not ask to be born; God placed me in this world, and now I feel adrift, wondering what my purpose is on earth. Why did God want my soul to come into my body at precisely this time, in this way? What did God intend for my soul to accomplish?

This is exactly what the soul is continually communicating to us, or trying to communicate to us: exactly how we are meant to improve the broken world. Its voice is not loud, like I imagine God's voice was at Mount Sinai. Rather, it is still and small, more like an intuition. At times, it guides us quietly, in small and measured steps. At other times, it seems to explode within, like a spiritual lightning bolt with amazing brightness and clarity.

Hearing the Call to Action

Hasidic lore refers to this voice of our soul as "a piece of God." It is hardwired within all humankind, an inner voice that is constantly inviting us to heal the world's brokenness. We naturally feel good whenever we actualize its message—so good, in fact, that we don't even need external positive feedback for our good deeds; we feel an inner reward.

We are spiritually wired to feel good after performing acts that make the world a better place.

I once asked a group of high school kids to share a moment when they felt best about themselves. I was surprised to hear story after story of kindnesses that they themselves had performed. Not one teenager shared a moment of great personal achievement: not dean's lists, touchdowns, and awards, but rather stories of giving, caring, and kindness. In retrospect, I realized that this should not have been a shock. We are spiritually wired to feel good after performing acts that make the world a better place. We receive an inner reward when we operate in tune with the voice of the soul.

> The voice of our soul communicates to us if we listen, telling us what we need to do to diminish the brokenness, to foster unity and wholeness.

According to Rav Kook, the song that our soul is always singing goes something like this: "Aryeh, this is your path, your purpose, your rightful destiny. This is what I brought you into the world to do. Aryeh, wake up and live your life. The world needs your unique contribution. Do it, do it now. Every day that you don't, the world will be lacking, and you will feel empty."

And Rav Kook goes further. He writes that learning Torah conditions me to be more attuned to my soul voice, that in fact this is the sole purpose of learning.[5] When learned soulfully, the wisdom of Torah can help me hear my calling in this world, help me navigate the great questions and countless small decisions I face every day.

In the music world, it is told that Mozart, a prolific prodigy who wrote symphonies from an early age, had difficulty getting out of bed in the morning. Legend has it that his mother would go to the piano and play an unresolved chord. This dissonance was so grating for the young genius that he had to get out of bed to resolve the discord. Similarly, it is the dissonance that we feel between what the world could be and what it is today that provokes us to action.

Grasping Our "Works-in-Progress-ness"

In the New Ager's pursuit of spirituality, there is significant emphasis on becoming present and at peace with the world. Often spiritually is equated with calm, serenity, and inner peace. "Jewish soulfulness," however, calls us in a different direction. We are here not to become at peace with the world as it is. Rather, the world is a work-in-progress that the voice of our soul urges us to heal.

Similarly, we ourselves are works-in-progress. Jewish soulfulness demands that we become fully present inside the real world's broken reality. We are enjoined to be outraged in the face of brokenness, sadness, and injustice. And then we are challenged to become partners with God in fixing it.

The voice of our soul communicates to us if we listen, telling us what we need to do to diminish the brokenness, to foster unity and wholeness. Indeed, as beings created in the image of God, our true partnership in creation is to help make this world reflect God's image.[6] So through a Jewish lens, soulfulness becomes:

- Being aware that I have a soul and that it is always communicating with me.
- Listening to the voice of my soul, a force yearning to create harmony in a broken world.
- Honoring my uniqueness while not placing myself at the center of the world.

The Challenge of the Voice of the Ego

Unfortunately, in addition to the voice of our soul, we have the competing voice of our ego, which complicates matters. The voice of the ego is usually loud and brash, making it difficult—and sometimes nearly impossible—to listen to the soul's still, small voice.

The ego voice is not focused on improving the world and re-creating paradise. It does not care about the brokenness of the world. The ego voice focuses on me alone and my personal story. Under the influence of the ego, I become the story. The ego voice:

- Urges us to assert that we are in full control of our lives, denying how vulnerable we actually are.
- Warns us to avoid risks, lest we fail.
- Tells us to be consumed with what others think of us, comparing ourselves to others and often judging them negatively at the same time.

Within each of us, an ongoing battle is raging between the soul voice and the ego voice, each trying to dominate. It is impossible to become a soulful being without recognizing the power and subtlety of the ego voice. The naïve among us imagine that the ego voice is present only in braggarts and conceited show-offs—only in those who seek the limelight. But the truth is that the ego voice is much more subtle than that; its voice is constantly whispering to us all.

For me personally, I know that my ego voice speaks especially loud and clear whenever I stand in front of the classroom. I continually hear it whispering:

- "Do the students like *me*?"
- "Do they respect *me*?"
- "Do they think *I* am deep enough?"
- "Am *I* smart enough?"
- "Do *I* know enough?"

Despite the fact that I truly, in my heart of hearts, believe that teaching is all about the students and not about me, my ego voice works overtime, albeit subtly, to make me focus on myself. It takes constant work and attention to stop being consumed with concern for what the students think of me.

The ego voice warns me against being spontaneous in the classroom, lest something not go perfectly and the students lose faith in me. It leads me to spin my story, speaking only of my highlights and strengths while hiding lesser moments and fears. It leads me to talk rather than to listen, to perform rather than to enable. In short, it keeps me focused on my own needs, not the needs of my students.

The ego voice severs the connection between our inner and outer lives. The Talmud relates to an upstanding person as someone who is *tocho k'voro*—a person whose "inside is like his outside" (Talmud, *Berachot* 28a). Originally, this characteristic was actually a requirement for being allowed to enter the *beit midrash*.

Becoming an authentic being, someone who is *tocho k'voro*, is extremely difficult. With whom can we ever be fully open, honest, and sincere? With whom can we let down our guard, making ourselves genuinely vulnerable? The incongruity of our inner and outer lives is impossible to avoid. We are fragile beings; when we express our issues, struggles, and disappointments, we put ourselves at risk. The world is not a safe place for total openness and is unwelcoming for our candidness and vulnerability. Isn't it significant that we often consider the people with whom we can fully share to be our "*soul* mates"?

But the real danger of the ego voice is not how we spin our lives to other people. Rather, it is our belief of the ego stories we tell ourselves, our unawareness that they are not really who we are. It can be scary to admit—especially to ourselves—that we are not in control of our lives, that we have experienced "downs" as well as "ups," and that we often feel confused, bewildered, and disheartened by the world and our actions.

It is difficult to understand and accept that God created a world with night as well as day, with darkness as well as light, and that our lives will flow with these cycles of shadow as well as clarity. To become a soulful being, I must become more aware of my inner voices, recognizing when I begin to let the ego voice take center stage, and then working to make myself *tocho k'voro*, to make my inside match my outside.

I recently spoke to a large group of adults at a conference. I started by saying, "I don't know any of you here. We have never met or spoken. But I'd be willing to bet that I already know something personal about each of you, which is something I also know about me—that there is some place in your life, in each of our lives, in which we are broken. Maybe it's a relationship, a job, your career, health, or finances. I'm willing to bet that there is not one person in this room who does not feel broken someplace in their life." Silence in the room, with several people nodding or smiling shyly. I would have won the bet. Then I continued, "But how many of you share this brokenness, even with your close friends and relatives?" A hush swept over the crowd. Life has taught us to be guarded and protective. We want to appear mature, successful, to have everything together. We present a nice façade, but it is never the whole truth.

> It is impossible to become a soulful being without recognizing the power and subtlety of the ego voice.

As to myself, when I listen to my inner truth, I begin to realize that my soul story:

- Often includes twists and turns, in which best-laid plans are undone by the unexpected.
- Is not afraid of change, fear, loss, failure, and shame, or mystery, passion, and ecstasy.
- Honors shadow as well as light, suffering as well as gladness.
- Connects me to myself, others, and God.

What Does It Mean to Be a Soulful Teacher?

E verything begins with the teacher.

Education thinker and activist Parker J. Palmer writes, "The transformation of teaching begins in the transformation of the heart of the teacher."[7] The heart of the teacher—not in the teacher's mind, and not in the teacher's teaching methods. Transformation is an inner process.

When I carry out faculty training programs, school principals often take me aside and say they want practical and immediate results. They tell me, "Don't linger too long on the theoretical stuff. Our staff won't have patience for that. They want *tachles* [practical applications—practical tips that they can use immediately]. If you talk abstractly or spiritually, you'll lose them."

I appreciate the need to address the immediate challenges of classroom teaching. But often, these pressing issues reflect deeper issues that arise from the soul-root at the heart of the educational system. To truly shift the classroom atmosphere, we have to shift its soul, and this requires a shift in the mind-set and the heart of the educator. And this is a process that takes time.

A year ago, I was teaching online to a group of four rabbis. They were together in a room next to the computer screen in the United States, and I was thousands of miles away from them, in Israel. This sort of teaching is very demanding; it is challenging to maintain the attention of the participants, and I was working hard to keep their focus. About twenty minutes into the session, they started passing notes to each other—I could see it clearly on the screen in front of me. I continued to teach but was feeling increasingly frustrated. Passing notes? A voice inside me said, "Have they reverted to fourth grade? I'm working hard and they're passing notes?"

After a few minutes the head rabbi put up his hand to stop me. He said, "Aryeh, I want to ask you a question. This soulful approach we're talking about: it seems to us that it isn't only for the classroom, but is really for everything that happens within the walls of our institution. The whole building should give off a sense of soulful space, and everyone—the staff, our administration, parents—everyone needs to be on board with this."

Bingo. I felt terrible about jumping to conclusions. The notes that they had been passing to each other were not a distraction; rather, they were an essential part of their process, their awakening. They understood that we were talking not about gimmicks or tricks but about a paradigm shift. They understood.

Of course teachers must assess their methodology, and tricks of the trade can definitely be used to address urgent and practical needs. But the real change that is required—indeed, the real change that is demanded, both by students and their teachers—is on a deeper level.

> To truly shift the classroom atmosphere, we have to shift its soul.

Most of today's teacher-training programs focus on the basic building blocks: mastery of a subject area, development of a clear and effective approach to pedagogy, and making the subject matter enjoyable (sometimes optional).

I have had the privilege of meeting many dedicated educators who have mastered these qualities. They know how to engage the class in a lively discussion, to organize projects, and to plan meaningful school outings. But when I ask, "What techniques do you use to get the students to go beyond their minds, to touch their *hearts* and *souls*?" they often look at me with blank stares.

Some teachers reject the question altogether, telling me that the classroom is the place for intellectual engagement and that spiritual and emotional support should be pursued in other settings. However, others quickly recognize the danger in such a bifurcated pedagogical approach. Do we really want to communicate the message that the truly meaningful questions—the depth and breadth of life itself—don't belong in the Jewish classroom?

Thinking this through often causes teachers to pause and contemplate the question again: "How can I evoke the souls of my students in my classroom? How can I bring the learning into my students' hearts?" When we discuss possible approaches, their answers generally fall into four categories:

- I have to be more passionate about what I teach.
- I have to tell more stories, to make the subject matter more personal and engaging.
- I should take the students out of the classroom more, to add variety to the experience.
- I should get us all to sing in the classroom—singing automatically takes us to a different level.

All of these answers are positive, and I spent years using them myself (until my students asked me to stop singing). However, as worthy as these approaches are, they are not sufficient, because they are not *evocative*. In these scenarios, I am, as the teacher, active, passionate—*I* am the story-teller, the singer. The students are passive, witnessing my performance. When I point this out to the teachers—that these approaches are focused on *them* while leaving the students in a passive role—they readily nod and acknowledge the problem.

Students need to become active in the classroom, with hearts and minds that are open, thinking, challenging, struggling.

Now is the time to go back to that rooftop, to shout my truth: "No one will ever be changed through a passive experience." Students need to become active in the classroom, with hearts and minds that are open, thinking, challenging, struggling. What is education worth if it does not evoke, elicit, and enable?

Harmonic Vibrations

So how does a normal teacher like you and me bring this sort of experience to the classroom? In my experience, it is surprisingly easy, once there has been a shift in mind-set. To this end, I humbly offer a radically different teaching approach that I call "harmonic vibrations."

Imagine two guitars facing each other. What happens when you pluck one guitar string on one of the guitars? Incredibly, a string on the other guitar begins to vibrate, all by itself. Even more incredibly, the string that vibrates is the same string that you plucked on the first guitar; that is, if you plucked the first string on one guitar, it is the first string of the facing guitar that will begin to vibrate on its own.

This is an amazing musical phenomenon, called harmonic or sympathetic vibration. What's even more amazing is that the same phenomenon exists within human beings. When we are in a group setting, we naturally and unconsciously shape our responses to the group's prevailing mood and tone.

Once, before the plenary session of a large conference, I walked over to a small group of people schmoozing and found that they were complaining that meetings like these are a waste of time. I found myself joining in, "Yeah, the speakers last year were so boring. I have so much to do and can't believe I'm going to waste so much time here. Ugh." I walked over to another group.

> The way to evoke the souls of my students is first to evoke my own soul, to pluck my soul string.

They were talking about the transportation nightmares that they had experienced on the way to the conference. I jumped in again, "Oh my God. My plane got stuck on the tarmac. We sat for two hours without water or air-conditioning. People were passing out, and I thought I was going to lose it."

Then I joined a third group, in which everyone was sharing a moment of kindness they had recently experienced. One mentioned that she had fallen asleep at the gate and would have missed her plane if a stranger hadn't noticed and woken her up. Another shared how kind the porter had been, and another how a neighbor had taken her to the airport at 3:00 a.m. after her car wouldn't start. After listening to a few stories, I added, "I took a taxi to the airport and raced into the terminal to grab my boarding pass. As I was waiting in line, I saw someone rushing over to me. It was the taxi driver! When the next client came into his cab he saw that my cell phone had slipped out of my pocket onto the floor of the cab. He refused the client, ran into the terminal, and found me. Amazing. I'm so grateful."

I had all three of these interactions in the space of just twenty minutes. One minute I was kvetching, the next moment I was grateful. How is this possible? Am I a chameleon? No, I am human, and this is how we work.

When the group I was in was complaining, they were plucking their own complaint strings, and this evoked a complaint from me, more or less automatically. And when the group told stories of gratitude, they were plucking their own gratitude strings, and this evoked my own gratitude.

In the book of Proverbs we read, "Like water, face-to-face" (27:19). When we look into water, we see our face reflected back to us. When I am with people, the face I present will evoke a similar response from them.

Plucking Your Soul String

Back to our question: "How can I evoke the soul of my students?" In countless classrooms, teachers are taking a harmonic vibrations approach to the challenge, and it is working. According to this model, the way to evoke the souls of my students is first to evoke my own soul, to pluck my soul string. When I evoke my own soul in the classroom, this naturally invites a matching response from my students.

Remember, the qualities that we said define a *soulful person* include:

- Being aware that I have a soul and that it is always communicating with me.
- Listening to the voice of my soul, a force yearning to create harmony in a broken world.
- Honoring my uniqueness while not placing myself at the center of the world.

A *soulful teacher* models this awareness in the classroom by:

- Sharing the uniqueness of his or her soul's journey with students.
- Sharing the yearning to become a better force for harmony.
- Sharing the hope that through learning, he or she will gain new clarity and take a small step in this direction.

How do I, the teacher, pluck my soul string?

- *Personal honesty:* I talk openly and honestly about why the subject is deeply meaningful to me and essential to my journey.
- *Work-in-progress:* I talk about how I am a work-in-progress and how this subject is critical to my personal growth and becoming my best self.

• *Futuristic:* I share my personal struggle regarding the topic—how I need to work on this aspect of my life and how our learning will hopefully be helpful for this.

For four years I was privileged to study with Israeli Bible scholar Nechama Leibowitz, one of the most influential Jewish teachers of our generation. Nechama liked to say that our students will forget everything we teach them but will remember our stories. Sharing my personal story—the fact that I want to continue growing, to become a more beneficial force in this world, and to use Jewish wisdom as the vehicle for healing this world—may be the most significant lesson I can offer my students.

In short, I am honest, open, sincere, and vulnerable. These qualities are not usually taught or stressed in teacher training programs because they are not essential for conveying subject matter and controlling a classroom. They are crucial, however, for fostering a personal connection to any subject and for bringing learning into life.

> If we want our students to become personally engaged with their learning, we need to demonstrate how we build a relationship with the subjects we learn.

A soulful educator exudes personal openness and a desire to grow personally.

When we walk into the classroom, we cannot help but exude the energy that drives us. A soulful educator exudes personal openness and a desire to grow personally. Often in my university and yeshiva experience, the professor or rabbi would walk into room and give the impression of being incredibly smart, a deep thinker, perhaps even a world-class scholar. Students usually responded by trying to ask the hardest question, to make the most insightful comment. They were reacting to the teacher's "plucking the smart string."

Soulful educators may be smart, but the model they want to project—the energy they want to exude—comes from a different place. They need to pluck the "open, personal, and vulnerable" string in order to evoke the same from their students.

The poet Marc Nepo writes about the source of the word "sincerity":

> If we trace the word—sincerity—we return to Roman times, where
> the Western form of the word originated. It comes from the Latin
> *sin cere*, meaning "without wax." During the Italian Renaissance,
> sculptors were as plentiful as plumbers, and markets selling marble
> and other stones were as prevalent as hardware stores. Frequently,
> stone sellers would fill the cracks in flawed stones with wax and
> try to sell them as flawless. Thus, an honest stone seller became
> known as someone who was *sincere*—one who showed his stone
> without wax, cracks and all.
>
> A sincere person, then, came to mean someone who is honest
> and open enough not to hide their flaws.[8]

I have found that this level of sincerity is hard for teachers to achieve in
their classrooms. We naturally want to present a "waxed" version of ourselves, to hide our flaws. Yet this actually distances our students from us. It
is actually the sharing of our flaws that endears us to our students.

Vulnerability researcher Brené Brown writes that vulnerability is often
confused with weakness, though it actually stems from courage. It takes
courage to be uncertain and to risk emotional exposure. Most adults are
averse to vulnerability; many have a great fear of being perceived as weak,
as lacking in control.

> The perception that vulnerability is weakness is the most widely
> accepted myth about vulnerability *and* the most dangerous. When
> we spend our lives pushing away and protecting ourselves from
> feeling vulnerable or from being perceived as too emotional, we
> feel contempt when others are less capable or willing to mask feel-
> ings, suck it up, and soldier on. We've come to the point where,
> rather than respecting and appreciating the courage and daring
> behind vulnerability, we let our fear and discomfort become judg-
> ment and criticism.[9]

Being vulnerable is not "letting it all hang out." It is not sharing without
boundaries. It is having the courage to acknowledge our imperfections and
to bring them, as part of our whole self, into everything we do, including
into our classroom.

This point cannot be emphasized too strongly: there is no relationship without vulnerability.

Sharing Our Works-in-Progress

If we want our students to become personally engaged with their learning, we need to demonstrate how we build a relationship with the subjects we learn. We do this by modeling how we personally engage with the subject, setting up harmonic vibrations that resonate within our students. I convey to the students that I am teaching this material because I am also a work-in-progress who wants and needs to grow and who believes that this learning will help me in my personal journey.

If we want our students to become personally engaged with their learning, we need to demonstrate how we build a relationship with the subjects we learn.

This pedagogical approach does not compromise the depth or seriousness of the material being taught. I am not asking teachers to sacrifice the intellectual rigor of their classrooms, to become wishy-washy or fluffy. Rather, it is about the *goal* of teaching. What do I really want to achieve?

- If I want students to open their hearts to the learning, then I have to model, to open my heart to the learning.
- If I want my students to be impacted by their learning, then I have to model, to be impacted by the learning.

This type of modeling is not a trick or gimmick, not a hook to grab attention. Sharing with my students why the subject is personally important for me—these are deep truths. I am, and will always be, a work-in-progress in every aspect of my life.

This approach radically changes the process of preparing a class. Before preparing to teach the subject matter itself, I need to wrestle with what I am teaching. I must pinpoint the *challenge* this subject brings up for me personally and then articulate it. My students will not personally wrestle with an issue if I have not wrestled with it myself. They will not engage with the subject more personally than I will. By "plucking my soul string," I am inviting students to allow the learning to enter their lives—to affect, develop, and enhance them.

We are not just talking about discovering the deep thought underlying our learning. Of course I want to understand the text in depth. But even more importantly, I want to be *personally affected* by it. The question is not "Do you understand the subject?" but rather "Now that you understand the subject, what does this subject mean to you? How does it impact your life?"

Soulful Education in Practice

How can this approach work in practice? Educators are often hesitant to begin personally modeling and framing the learning before diving into the actual material to be taught. Typical complaints include:

- It will take too much time; there won't be enough left to cover the syllabus.
- This is not an appropriate approach for every subject.
- This can be overdone. There can be too much sharing.

Too Much Time

How much time does it take to personally model and frame a subject? Probably less than ten minutes. When introducing this idea to teachers, I often refer to it as the "spice" of their teaching. The spice of any cooking is only 2 or 3 percent, but without any seasoning, the food will be tasteless. If it has too much, it will probably be inedible. The "harmonic vibration" introduction should not take too long and should certainly not overshadow the material being taught. But without the introduction, the lessons will end up being tasteless.

Not Appropriate for Every Subject

I would have no idea how to apply this approach to mathematics (although an Ayeka graduate recently informed us that she is incorporating Soulful Education into her university-level statistics classes). But it is not difficult for most teachers to find ways to express how the ideas of Judaic studies, humanities, and most sciences are personally meaningful and relevant to them.

During a recent training session, three teachers challenged me to "Ayeka-cize" their subjects. How would I introduce and model harmonic vibrations in history, Talmud, prayer? Well, there are as many answers as there are teachers. But I was willing to offer what my own personal responses might be today, with the knowledge that they could be completely different tomorrow, or the next day, or the next.

A history teacher asked how I would frame the teaching of World War II. I checked in with myself, and this is what came up:

> What strikes me especially about this war were the innumerable acts of heroism. Not just the soldiers who received medals and were cited for exceptional bravery, but the small acts of courage that happened all the time. The moments when soldiers were afraid, hesitated, and then acted. The moments when commanders were terrified to make a decision, knowing how much was at stake, and then nevertheless followed through. The countless times people who were *behind* the front lines chose to step up and get involved, even though they could have remained on the sidelines.
>
> I am very excited that we are going to study this now because "stepping up" has never been easy for me. I have found it much easier to let someone else take action. But I have always wanted to be more of a "step-up guy." Recently I saw some kids litter, throw their lunch garbage on the side of a hill, and what did I do? Nothing. I didn't step up; I stood by. I let it go. It was much easier not to step up. I hesitated and the moment was lost.
>
> So I'm really looking forward to studying about World War II with you, because even at my old age I am looking forward to taking a small step to becoming a bit braver. I really hope that by doing this learning I will be inspired by what we see and think about. I hope to personally grow through learning this subject with you.

How about Talmud? A high school Talmud teacher was looking for a way to make the eighth chapter of *Sanhedrin*, which discusses whether a person is allowed to kill or wound someone who is breaking into his home, relevant for his students. Once again, I checked in with myself, and this is what came up:

> For the next few months we will be focusing on *haba b'machteret*— how we should act when someone breaks into our property. Thank

God, I have never been in this situation. But if I were, what do I have to take into consideration? Are there any limits on what I am allowed to do to the other person in order to protect myself? Do I still have to consider the humanity of the other person? To what degree?

There are plenty of situations in which we feel invaded, and there are many ways to kill or wound someone without attacking them physically. If we embarrass or neglect someone, in that moment we take away their dignity and kill a part of them. Everyone is created in the image of God. I can easily compromise this "image" without shedding blood.

Just yesterday, I had a very confusing moment, and I didn't know what to do. I was riding the subway and was the only person left in the car. A guy in his forties entered from the previous car, obviously drunk. He called over to me, asking if I had a cigarette. I answered "no" and began to feel very uncomfortable. He came closer, right up to me, inches away from my face, and asked me for some money.

He didn't break into my home, but I felt that he was invading my personal space, and I just wanted to get out of the situation. I was thinking only of myself. But then I sensed this person also was created in the image of God, and if I ignored or belittled him, then for a moment would I be slightly "killing" him? I thought, do I give him some money? How do I give it to him—begrudgingly, kindly? What do I do?

> The question is not "Do you understand the subject?" but rather "Now that you understand the subject, what does this subject mean to you? How does it impact your life?"

My personal space was broken into—how do I respond? There are so many times when I feel someone has, intentionally or unintentionally, violated my personal space. I don't want to react automatically, unthinkingly. I don't want to react in anger or revenge. Precisely at these situations I want my "best self" to be on duty.

I'm going to keep this story in mind as we study this tractate together. I wish I had had the clarity to know what to do yesterday. A thousand thoughts went through my mind, but in the end I was a mass of confusion. I'm okay with that right now, since I realize that I am a work-in-progress, even at my age. I'm looking forward to gaining insight from Jewish wisdom so that when a scenario like this recurs, I'll have a better sense of how to act and respond.

And prayer? A high school teacher was looking for a way to teach the concept of *Sh'viti HaShem l'negdi tamid*, "I place God in front of me always," without putting his students to sleep.

I asked, "If you were to grade yourself, from 1 to 10, on your own success at keeping God in front of you always, what number would you give yourself?" He thought for a moment, and then said, "A 5." I asked him if he shared this with his students. His eyes popped open, and I could see that he was thinking this through.

I said, "I bet you are thinking something like 'How can I share that I am not perfect at this? I'm the rabbi, and I'm supposed to have figured this all out and have it down pat. What would happen if I exposed myself and shared that I am still working on this part of Jewish life?'" He nodded.

I checked in with myself and offered:

> Today we are going to study one of the most challenging ideas in all of Judaism. It's only four words, but for me it captures the heart of what it really means to be a Jew, and I have to admit that I'm struggling with it. We're going to talk about placing God continually in front of us, *Sh'viti HaShem l'negdi tamid*. A simple four words but, for me, a huge challenge. I would say that on a scale of 1 to 10, I'm probably usually about a 5 at doing this. I have some better days and some worse days, but on the whole, I'm not sure that I would give myself a passing grade. This is a very hard thing to do, and I guess I have not focused on it enough.
>
> I think it is about time for me to face this challenge and figure out what has been holding me back from doing this better and what steps I could take to better live this idea. I really hate to just say words of the prayer book that I am not actually doing. It makes

me feel fake and inauthentic, that I am just giving lip service to these amazing ideas. This is a huge opportunity for me to tackle this issue head-on.

What number would you all give to yourselves, on a scale of 1 to 10, regarding *Sh'viti HaShem l'negdi tamid*?

All three teachers—history, Talmud, and prayer—acknowledged that framing the learning in this way would not take up too much time and would not detract from the learning. In fact, by connecting to the material themselves in this way, they would become more excited and engaged with the subject.

Soulful Education contends that every era of history, every section of Talmud, every part of the prayer book, and all other subjects can be framed in an open, personal, and life-enhancing way.

> Soulful Education contends that every era of history, every section of Talmud, every part of the prayer book, and all other subjects can be framed in an open, personal, and life-enhancing way.

Too Much Sharing

You may ask, can this kind of framing be overdone? Absolutely. The art of this technique is in the balance. As I mentioned before, framing is the "spice" and should be just 2 to 3 percent of the overall learning. I suggest that teachers give "frames" to every subject, not every class. As each subject is introduced—a new era in history, a new *sugya* (section) in Talmud, or a new unit in Torah, prayer, ethics—it should be personally framed to give it a lens through which the entire learning will be viewed. When the next broad subject is tackled, it is time for the next frame.

Learning How to Be Open, Vulnerable, and a Work-in-Progress in the Classroom

While working with educators during the last several years, I have been surprised—and not surprised—to discover just how difficult it is for many to begin "plucking their soul string" for their students. Surprised because this is not rocket science. After the educators grasp and affirm the need to bring a personal dimension to the classroom, it seems like it should be easy for them to begin being honest and authentic. How hard is it to bring oneself into the classroom?

And not surprised because virtually none of the educators that I meet has ever had a teacher who modeled this style of teaching for them. In my own many years at university and yeshiva, I never had a teacher or rabbi talk openly, personally, or vulnerably. It is very difficult to shed the styles of education that we ourselves grew up with.

Most of the challenges faced by educators as they begin to personally model in the classroom fall into one of four categories: not talking in the first person, talking too generally, fear of admitting weakness, and feeling like a fraud.

Not Talking in the First Person

It is essential but incredibly difficult to use the first person in an educational setting. Most educators I've encountered are reluctant to "pluck their soul string" and instead prefer to speak in collective terms, such as "People tend to …," "We often …," "You should consider…." This is a protective mechanism—protecting oneself from vulnerability. In addition, from our college essay days, many of us have been conditioned to remove the "I" from any serious intellectual effort. In my many years in the *beit midrash*, I never spoke in the first person; the language we used was "The Gemara says" or "Rambam asserts." It is ironic that our adult learning taught us to give up our personal voice.

Initially, I was self-conscious about talking about myself in the classroom. Questions kept popping up in the back of my head: "Aryeh, is this intellectually rigorous? Does anyone else really care what you think? Aren't you supposed to teach the books and not bring yourself into this? Is this becoming about you? Are you being narcissistic?"

But there is no way to "pluck my own soul string" other than to talk about my own experience in my own voice. It takes a lot of practice to feel comfortable opening up.

Talking Too Generally

Consider the following introduction that a community rabbi gave for a class on prayer:

Prayer is a difficult subject. Many people struggle with prayer. I, too, have had moments when prayer was hard for me. There have been times when I wrestled with my belief in God. Many great thinkers in our history also have struggled with different parts of the prayer service.

The rabbi thought he was being personal and vulnerable, but he was actually being quite guarded. He spoke in general terms, without specifying exactly what his struggles were or when they occurred. He didn't give his students anything to grab onto, any opening for a further conversation. He talked "about" his situation, without entering into it. By leaving out the *what* and *why*, he made it difficult to believe in the authenticity of the experience or for the students to feel a sense of connection with his struggle.

It would have been far more effective if the rabbi had detailed a particular time or prayer that was challenging for him, sharing precisely how he was struggling with it and why. If he had explained what, when, and why this prayer was causing him to rethink a portion of his life, all with as much detail as possible, the students would naturally identify with him and begin to connect more personally with the material studied.

At one point in my career, I often took students on visits to Yad Vashem, Jerusalem's Holocaust Memorial Museum. Passing through exhibit after exhibit of spirit-numbing horror—all documented to the smallest detail with testimonies, images, artifacts, art, documents, and more—the experience can be overwhelming. To help the students focus, I suggested that each person look for a single snapshot while going through the exhibit—a single element that truly resonated with them—and to hold the image in their minds to share later with the group. The experience of Yad Vashem as a whole was too overwhelming to grasp. But each of us could manage to focus on a single object, a single thought. This focus enhanced our ability to experience the whole.

This focus is the key to success in "plucking our soul string" in front of our students. We choose one string, we focus on one moment, and we make that one element come alive with as much detail as possible. We don't share general, formless accounts of the personal struggle; rather, we describe it as specifically and as fully as possible. The sharper the "plucking of the soul string," the more evocative it becomes for the listeners.

Fear of Admitting Weakness

Recently a rabbi said to me, "How can I share my doubts or struggles? I am the rabbi, an ambassador for Judaism! People expect me to have the answers. I can't disappoint them."

The ludicrous part of his admission was that he was a new teacher, only twenty-eight years old. Does anyone really expect a twenty-eight-year-old to have all of the answers? But this was the role he felt he needed to play.

I have found this to be one of the greatest and most poignant fears of rabbis and educators: "I should have the answers." Lurking behind this proclamation is the nagging fear, "If I do not have the answers, if I do not know how to answer every question, will I communicate that Judaism doesn't have all the answers? Or that I am a fraud? Will the students and congregants consider me illegitimate? What will happen to my position?" The tragic irony here is that precisely the opposite will happen if educators talk personally and share their struggle.

> Gnawing self-doubt eats away at every rabbi, teacher, and educator I know. No one ever believes that he or she knows enough.

A high school principal related to me that students go to their general studies teachers when they need to talk, not to their Gemara teachers. When he asked them why, they said it was because the Gemara teachers presented themselves as having all of the answers, with no questions or doubts. They gave the impression that they weren't struggling with anything.

The students said that this was a very distancing and unrelatable model. They were filled with questions, and these teachers only had answers. A few students commented that they felt these teachers were not really being authentic with them, that they were playing a role they thought they were supposed to play, appearing to be authorities with full certainty. Students felt that these teachers were "spinning it." They wanted to approach only the teachers who were honest and sincere with them.

Educators have told me that their students are desperate to get to know them. They leap at any personal incident or story. Rather than disrespecting them for sharing their authentic questions, the students will admire and appreciate them more for their acknowledgments.

Furthermore, sharing with our students is possibly the greatest way of honoring them. A student recently said to me, "When the teacher shares something from her personal life with us, I feel she is treating us as equals, that she is bringing us into her inner circle. She becomes much more real and accessible. Now I would even consider approaching her outside of class with an issue."

Feeling Like a Fraud

It took me way too long to become a full person in my classroom. As a person who only "discovered" Judaism in my twenties, I always felt that other teachers knew more than I did, and I suffered acute bouts of insecurity. I lived in fear that others would discover just how little I actually knew and that I would be exposed as a fraud. I have found that I am not alone in these panic-stricken feelings.

> Sharing with our students is possibly the greatest way of honoring them.

I was once asked to offer helpful pointers to fifteen rabbinical students during the last weeks of their training. I opened by asking a straightforward question: "Okay, rabbis-to-be, how many of you are scared to death that you don't know enough?" Every hand shot up like a rocket. It was as if they had put their hands into an electric socket. They couldn't raise their hands high enough.

And then I asked them, "And when do you think you will know enough? When will that happen?"

A long pause.

"Do you know," I continued, "that your rabbi also thinks he doesn't know enough? And his rabbi's rabbi also. And his rabbi's rabbi's rabbi! It never ends."

This anxiety was palpable for these future rabbis. They had devoted endless hours to their learning. Their personal self-esteem as well as their future career success was entirely dependent on their ability to prove their intellectual proficiency and expertise. They defined themselves as knowledgeable educators. And they were plagued with doubts.

What happens to a rabbi or teacher who feels that he or she does not know enough? What happens to the inner psyche of an educator who questions his or her authenticity; who is plagued by feelings that he or she is a fraud?

This gnawing self-doubt eats away at every rabbi, teacher, and educator I know. No one ever believes that he or she knows enough. There are always more unopened books, more insights, more sources; people who are smarter, more experienced, wiser. A Soulful Education perspective helps us overcome these fears. My fears are, after all, the clever ploys of my ego voice. They are all about *me*.

For an educator, the ego often surfaces in self-doubts. Every time teachers enter a class, they risk being deflated, neglected, or scoffed at by the students. One withering look from a student can squash a self-image. One look of boredom or disdain can lead to endless thoughts of uncertainty and insecurity.

The ego voice is continually whispering, "Do the students like *me*? Do they respect *me*? Am *I* smart enough? Deep enough? Funny and interesting enough?" The ego voice focuses on me—the teacher—and not the students.

Soulful Education is about replacing this ego voice with the voice of the soul that is saying, "It is not about me. How can I best serve my students?"

Creating Soulful Space

The first task in Soulful Education is to create an environment of safe space that is soul friendly. By "safe space" we mean an environment in which we respect a person's soul. We neither invade nor disregard a person's inner life. Our interest in other people is driven by our desire to make them feel valued and supported, and not by our own curiosity. In the words of the poet Rainer Maria Rilke, "We stand at the border of the other's soul and salute it."[10]

Safe space is very rare today. It does not exist in most places of work or study. For most people it does not exist even in their home environment. Even people who know us well often hold expectations regarding our roles and behavior. These expectations can lead us to play a certain character, where stepping out of our role would make everyone uncomfortable, perhaps even worried.

It is not easy to talk about our personal beliefs and behaviors. Often we fear being judged by others, anxious that we will become less in their eyes. We carefully guard what we share and with whom, building walls around the more vulnerable parts of our lives.

So where can we safely explore our beliefs, hopes, fears, and aspirations? If these are not shared, will they begin to fade and become forgotten? How will we continue to grow if we cannot venture beyond this threshold? With whom can we share these fragile inner parts? In what environment is sincere sharing possible? The answer: only in an environment of unconditional acceptance, in which we are accepted for our very beings and not for our achievements.

Staking Fertile Ground for the Inner Voice

Poets have described the soul as being shy, ready to emerge from an inner place of hiding only if there is no fear of being wounded or ignored. Safe space allows for emotional expression and honesty.

Safe space is an essential component of Ayeka sessions. It is necessary because as facilitators, we are not engaging simply in conveying information or teaching skills. We are trying to create a space that allows everyone in the group to speak from an inner voice. If we do not create such a setting, then there is little chance of our workshops being personally meaningful or successful.

With safe space there is:

- No cynicism
- No judging
- No attacking or criticizing
- No discrediting
- No need to be defensive

With safe space people can:

- Deeply listen to and support one another.
- Value each individual's unique decisions and path in life.
- Guard the privacy and integrity of each other's inner life.
- Express their successes and failures, their dreams and their anxieties, their momentous and embarrassing moments.
- Share words and solitude with similar equanimity.

Safe space enables us to let down our guard without concern that we will be wounded or neglected.

The Mind Versus the Soul

Most educational environments are not safe spaces; they thrive on debate that can sometimes become angry and bitter. The *beit midrash* is known for especially brutal arguments. The Talmud refers to two people studying together as "beating each other" to sharpen their thinking. I remember my study partner, Daniel, and me often screaming at each other while we studied Gemara. There was an utter disregard for our feelings and sensitivities. The goal was to sharpen and deepen our understanding. The intensity and sharpness of our disagreements did usually lead to a deeper comprehending of our subject. We loved to argue, debate, and attack. I often felt a visceral rush during our intellectual confrontations. Adrenaline would flow as we poised to intellectually spar with each other.

But the soul engages differently than the mind. It is fragile and shy, like an amoeba. In ninth-grade biology, I learned that when an amoeba is attacked, it withdraws into itself and firms up its walls. Our souls act the same way—they withdraw from conflict and judgment.

It is not easy to engage personally. We fear being judged by others, anxious that we will come up lacking. We carefully guard what we share and with whom, building walls around the more vulnerable parts of our lives. We are easily bruised. We need to put up guards in our lives to safeguard the fragility and preciousness of our soul.

At the beginning of my teaching career, I once taught a class on Jewish prayer to a group of twenty adults. One woman shared sincerely and personally about her own experience of prayer. Another participant, who was sitting directly across from her in the circle and was in full view of the other students, rolled her eyes. This hurtful gesture lasted only a fraction of a second, but everyone saw it. Because of that one moment, everyone else in the group immediately closed down, not daring to engage emotionally or personally. They all continued to engage with their minds, but not with their hearts. It was way too dangerous. No one wanted to risk becoming the next target of rolling eyes. Needless to say, the woman who had shared something personal was crushed.

One moment of rolling eyes shut down the whole group. I wondered to myself, how long will the group be emotionally shut down? How long will it take for the withering effect of the rolling eyes to wear off?

Despite my optimism and, apparently, youthful naiveté, it soon became clear to me that the group would continue to be emotionally and spiritually closed for the entirety of our remaining time together. The breaking of safe space never naturally wears off. The participants continued to engage intellectually, they asked questions and offered insightful comments, but no one risked being personally open or engaged.

This tragic truth often infuriates me: it is almost impossible for one person to raise the level of a whole group, but it is incredibly easy for one person to bring down the whole group. In just a few seconds, the "rolling-eyes" participant succeeded in shutting down the whole group for all of our time together.

Looking back now, it is clear to me what I should have done to fix the situation, but at the time I was utterly clueless. I should have paused the conversation and, in the most respectful way, said to the rolling-eyes participant, "I know that you would never intentionally hurt someone, but it is painful to be the object of rolling eyes. We need to maintain a space in which everyone can express their opinions without fear of judgment." I imagine that she would have then apologized, and we could have carried on.

Establishing Ground Rules

How can we create an environment of safe space in our classrooms? How is it possible to sustain a learning setting bereft of cynicism, judgment, and attacking? Well, contrary to what I originally thought, I have found—to my delight and disbelief—that it can actually be easy to create and sustain safe space.

On my first day in a class I simply announce that we are invoking a safe space environment for the duration of our learning together. I pass out a page describing safe space and ask the students if anyone has a problem with the guidelines. This document serves as our contract for our time together.

To my surprise, students have loved this opportunity to free them from having to maintain a cool or intellectual veneer. It freed them from worrying about rolling eyes or disparaging comments. They really didn't always want to hide behind a shell of cynicism or to remain aloof. I have never needed to enforce the safe space rules. The students have been zealous to maintain the group's integrity.

An experienced high school teacher once said to me that he was struggling with cynical comments in his classroom. I asked him if he allowed his students to beat each other up physically in his classroom. "Of course not," he replied. "That's a no-brainer." Then I asked him, "Then why do you allow cynicism? Isn't that a form of beating up, just verbally instead of physically? Isn't that a form of stealing, since it takes away from other students the opportunity to be fully engaged, to be themselves in the classroom?"

I often made the mistake of focusing so much on the material that I loved and wanted to teach that I ignored the social dynamics of the classroom. For years I taught Talmud. One year I had a student who spoke a bit too loudly and a bit too long in class. It often grated on the other students. I remember one class vividly. I was writing on the board and had my back to the students. The student was making a point, a bit too loudly and a bit too long. All of a sudden, a woman in the class burst out, "Are you ever going to finish? You're driving me nuts!"

I froze. My hand was on the blackboard; I stopped writing mid-sentence. I remember the panicked thoughts racing through my mind: "What should I do now? That outburst was so cutting and devastating. What is he thinking now? What is she thinking now? What should I do?"

And then I did the worst thing possible. I ignored what happened. I said to myself, "Aryeh, you're not a social worker or therapist. You don't need to get involved in the social dynamics of your class. You're a teacher. That's what you know how to do, and that's what you are here for. Don't get involved." So I turned to the class and said, "Can we get back to learning, to the Gemara? Let's focus."

That was the worst possible thing I could have done. I was giving my students the educational message that the content of learning was more important than our moral behavior; that the words on the page were more important than the people in the room. Needless to say, after this eruption, the students could not concentrate and certainly would not engage personally.

I was once invited to teach a class of seventeen-year-old boys in New York City. I started the class by announcing that over the next ninety minutes we were going to be functioning in a cynicism-free zone. If they wanted to stay in the class, they would have to dock their cynicism at the door. One kid looked at me and said, "You just asked me to take off my whole personality. I'm a cynic. If I take it off, you'll just have a bunch of bones sitting in front of you."

I wouldn't budge. I told him that outside of class he could be as cynical and sarcastic as he wanted, but the rule inside was support and respect. Sixty minutes later, this same (formerly cynical) seventeen-year-old boy wrote a personal and heart-wrenching poem that I still have. When given the chance to take off his protective armor, he sincerely and heartfully engaged.

This is the opportunity we need to give to all of our students. Safe space will never just happen. We need to intentionally construct safe space for our students, so they may let down the guards they carry and open their hearts to our teaching.

The Soulful Education Approach

Loving Our Students

The most important quality of a teacher is to love his or her students—all of them. This may be the most important realization I have had in my long and winding teaching career.

I recently met with a group of young professionals who are pursuing master of education degrees. I asked them a simple question: "On a scale of 1 to 10, what number would you give yourself regarding how you much you care for your students?" As soon as I finished the question, a collective groan emerged from most of the soon-to-be teachers. They started calling out numbers: "5, 6, maybe 7 on a good day." "3½."

But their looks spoke volumes. It was clear that the question had struck a raw nerve. They felt guilty that they didn't like their students more. They intuitively understood that caring for students is probably the most basic and significant role of a teacher. Yet something was preventing them from getting there.

I was surprised, even slightly baffled. "No one forced you to go into education. You are all young and talented and could have entered any profession you wanted. Why did you choose to be teachers if you can't say that you love your students?"

One said, "I really like most of them. It's just that a few of them wipe me out, and then I want to throw them out of the class. But then, I always feel guilty as I remember that I was one of those kids and that I always wished my teacher would have treated me differently."

Another said, "I'm just not an emotional guy. Even though I'm older than my students, they often intimidate me. I worry that I won't be able to control the class well enough. They destroy my self-image."

A third said, "I don't want to show them that I care about them. I try to be strong, hard, and disciplined to establish my authority. People told me that I shouldn't smile till January."

Sometimes It's Difficult to Love

The truth is, it is very difficult to love, or at least like, all of our students, all of the time. Some students are blessed with natural qualities that make them easy to like. It may be their personality, their looks, or even their quirkiness. They are the fortunate ones.

But I have found that in every teaching setting, there are always a few students who, for some reason, are much more challenging to like, to be patient with, and to care for. For some, the formal educational setting is not conducive to their strengths. For others, it can be a personality trait, mood swings, or even the sound of their voice. With these students, it is much more challenging to be sensitive to what they really need, to listen to what is not being said and what is being said between the lines.

For us as teachers, this presents a huge quandary, as we know that these students are not getting what they need from us. We are not actually doing anything negative, but the disconnection is palpable and will inevitably lead to disengagement.

Finding the Path to Loving

For the astute and caring teacher, this flawed relationship is disturbing. Even with this lack of bonding, teachers can probably teach information successfully, but the experience remains empty and deflating. In addition, for caring teachers the lack of connection brings guilt and a sense of failure to perform up to the high standards of their sacred calling.

This lack of connection is, of course, not a new phenomenon. One of the most familiar verses in the Torah instructs us to love/like those in our presence:

> You should not take revenge, nor hold a grudge toward any of your people, you should like/love your neighbor as yourself, I am God. (Leviticus 19:18)

It is interesting to note the full message of this verse. The most recognized part of the verse, "You should love your neighbor as yourself," does not stand alone. This phrase could have been considered a full independent verse, but instead it is the concluding and culminating segment of a deeper thought. Only in the context of "You should not take revenge, nor hold a grudge" does this command of loving really have an impact. We are not commanded to love those whom we naturally or already care for. For our friends and family, we need no external instruction to care—the desire for a close bond comes naturally.

> **The most important quality of a teacher is to love his or her students—all of them.**

Rather, it is the people we want to harm, take revenge on, or carry a grudge about that the Torah tells us we need to love. We are mandated to love the people we dislike. How is it possible to do this? How is it possible to consciously change how we feel toward someone? How is it possible to teach and train ourselves to care for those we hate, especially if we hate them for a good reason?

Jewish thinkers present four archetypal methods for rising to this challenge and developing closeness for someone who at present is held distant.

Hirsch: Love as an Action

Samson Raphael Hirsch, a leading nineteenth-century rabbi in Western Europe, offers us a behavioral approach for fulfilling the directive of loving our fellow person. He writes in his commentary on the verse in Leviticus:

> "You should love (to) your neighbor as yourself" is the final summarizing axiom for the whole of our social behavior, in feelings, word and deed. The noblest fundamental feeling toward God and man is love.... Now here it does not say: "You should love your neighbor as yourself" as it does everywhere else. That would entail the loving of the *person* of our neighbor as we love ourselves, which is practically impossible to carry out, and the demand in the Torah is for such love to be given to all our fellow people. Such complete sympathetic harmony of two natures in every direction is only seldom to be found....

But what it does say here is "You will love *to* your fellow person like yourself" and this is not the person himself, but everything that pertains *to the person*, all the conditions of his life, the wealth and affliction which make up his position in the world. To this we are to give our love as if it were our own. We are to rejoice in his good fortune and grieve over his misfortune as if it were our own. We are to assist at everything that furthers his well-being and happiness as if we were working for ourselves. We must keep trouble away from him as assiduously as if it threatened ourselves. This is something that does lie within our possibilities and is something that is required of us even toward somebody whose personality may be actually highly distasteful to us. For the demand of this love is something which lies quite outside the sphere of the personality of our neighbor. It is not based on any of his qualities.[11]

Hirsch is sensitive to the emotional impossibility of actually loving everyone. The Torah never commands us to do something beyond our capabilities. Love is not something I can simply engineer on demand. As all emotions, it is susceptible to the whims and vicissitudes of life. Just because I am told to love someone does not mean that I can actually engender this feeling in my heart.

For Hirsch, the love commanded in the Torah is not an emotion, but an action. The Torah does not command me to love my fellow being in my heart; rather, the Torah commands me to act and behave as if I love him or her. Hirsch bases his approach on a very close reading of the Hebrew grammar of the verse. "But what it does say here is 'You will love *to* your fellow person [*l'rei'echa*] like yourself.'" The Hebrew *l'* (to) precedes *rei'echa* (your neighbor). Behaving with love is something entirely within my control. It is, for Hirsch, in my hands and actions.

Of the four approaches enumerated here, I have often considered Hirsch's approach to be the most accessible. It is not contingent upon the vagaries of my inner life. I simply have to behave as a mensch. I have to help and be attentive, even when I'm not in the mood. There may be a deep disconnect between my external behavior and my internal state of being; I may be smiling on the outside while grimacing on the inside. Nevertheless, it is possible to achieve this degree of control. According to this interpretation, the summoning of the external effects of affinity—behavior that "mimics" kindheartedness—represents the minimal level of caring that all students deserve.

Maimonides: Love as a Function of Knowing

Maimonides offers a different approach to developing feelings of love. We can extrapolate from his words regarding the development of a loving relationship with God how we should go about developing a loving relationship with other people.

> It is a clear and known thing that one's love for God is not fully developed in one's heart unless one is fittingly lovesick always and leaves everything in this world except for God. As is stated in the verse: "You shall love the Lord your God with all of your heart, all of your soul, and all of your might." A person can only love God by virtue of the knowledge that one knows God. According to the level of knowledge will be the level of one's love: if a little—then a little; if a lot—then a lot. Therefore one must direct oneself to understand, analyze, know, and be wise in the ways that convey wisdom of God. Everyone according to one's strength that one has to understand and grasp the Creator.[12]

For Maimonides, loving is a function of knowledge. Unlike Hirsch, for Maimonides it is actually possible to engender feelings of love, to even become lovesick. The commandment to love is really a commandment to increase one's knowledge of the other, to know the other better.

Often our disconnection from another stems from the fact that we do not fully understand them or their situation. Our responses to the other are based on our very limited knowledge of them. We never have the full picture of anyone else, even those we are closest to. So how can we, as teachers, believe that we fully know any of our students? We rarely have awareness of even the most external fundamentals, like what the student's home life and family structure look like.

Often our disconnection from another stems from the fact that we do not fully understand them or their situation.

Often during staff meetings at the beginning of the year, the teachers would discuss the students and sometimes comment on how challenging some of them are. Then, after the teacher-parent meetings, we would meet and in almost perfect unison proclaim, "Now I understand why they behave like that." Meeting the parents gave greater insight into the personality traits of the children. While this may not have led directly to love, it usually increased our level of patience and sympathy.

I often think that if Maimonides were guiding our teachers today, he would recommend simply taking the time to talk—and especially to listen—to the students we are having the hardest time connecting with. He would encourage us to find out what they like to do, what their family situation is, whatever else is going on with them. The more we know them, the more our hearts may open.

Sefat Emet: Love as Cultivated Within

A completely different approach to fulfilling "love your neighbor as yourself" is offered by the great Hasidic master the Sefat Emet, in his commentary on the Torah:

> The philosophers challenge this idea [of being able to love on demand] and say: "How is it possible to command love? Isn't love an abstract idea which is dependent on the nature of the person; can a person love simply by virtue of being thus commanded?"
>
> However, the answer is inherent in the question. Because the verse commands us to love, we must conclude that it is potentially possible for each individual to love, if only he does what is necessary to arouse this love.
>
> And this, in fact, is the essence of the commandment: that one should perform whatever actions are necessary to stimulate these latent feelings of love that are within.[13]

For the Sefat Emet, this verse conveys a startling thought: we actually can control and evoke the emotion of love on demand.

Unlike Hirsch, who presumed that it was impossible to love everyone and therefore could not be commanded, the Sefat Emet comes to the opposite conclusion: we would have thought that loving everyone is impossible if not for the command in the verse. The Torah is teaching us something we never would have thought possible: we actually do have the inner wherewithal to have love in our hearts for all people.

According to the Sefat Emet, we are hard-wired to love. The urge to connect with all of humanity is a fundamental part of each of us, even if it is asleep most of the time. We can arouse this dormant potential through conscious and intentional effort.

Unlike Hirsch or Maimonides, for the Sefat Emet, loving the other is not dependent on the quality of our relationship. Rather, it is an inner process that takes place completely within myself. The verse in Leviticus is instructing me to work on myself, to make myself a more loving human being. I need to increase my capacity to love, to "stretch the muscles of my heart."

When I encounter students who are challenging to connect with, it is as if they are messengers relaying a wake-up call. They are sending me a message—from God?—that I need to work on myself and to become a more compassionate and caring person. While I will never fulfill my end-less potential for loving, these students are a reminder—an incentive—to continue to actively work on opening my heart and expanding my capacity for kindheartedness.

Kook: Love as Sanctioned and Sustained Through God

Each of these three approaches to becoming a more loving person and to loving students focuses on a different aspect of the three primary dimen-sions of human nature—the mind, heart, and body. For Hirsch, the locus of loving is our actions. For Maimonides, it is our thoughts. For the Sefat Emet, it is our emotions.

For Rav Abraham Isaac Kook, it is our souls. Rav Kook writes:

> Who can stop the supreme light of Divine love, which beats in the heart of the pure and righteous?
>
> All of the Torah, ethical behavior, mitzvot, actions and Talmudic learning come to clear the path from the obstacles of loving, to enable this infinite love to expand and embrace all of the spheres of life.
>
> It is impossible for one to not be filled with love for every crea-ture, since the light of the Divine blessing shines in every thing and every thing is the revealing of the beauty of God. God's loving kindness fills the earth.[14]

For Rav Kook there is a spiritual imperative to love everything. Elsewhere he writes:

> It is impossible not to be filled with love for all of creation, since the ever-flowing light of God shines through everything, and everything is the revealing of the sweetness of divine beauty. God's kindness fills the world.[15]

Loving is not something I need to work on. I do not need to struggle or to plan to engender loving. Loving is not dependent on my relationship with anyone else; it is the natural and reciprocal response to a world that was created by God's love and that continues to be sustained through God's love. Every element of creation has infinite value, as it was brought into existence by none other than the Creator.

If I am having a difficult time connecting with and caring for students, I need to remind myself that, first and foremost, they were created by God and carry God's light in them through their souls. If I distance myself from them, it is as if I am denying their transcendent nature. This, of course, does not mean that I need to agree with or validate their actions. But for Rav Kook, the holiness and intimacy of connection with every human being are sacrosanct and inviolable.

Four approaches, four strategies to utilize in the quest to love our students. Which of these approaches is correct? Mind, heart, body, or soul? Needless to say, they each possess an element of truth and can assist us in our endless pursuit of becoming more loving teachers.

The Soulful Paradigm: Mentoring from Love

Soulful Education requires that we love our students and posits several paradigm shifts in how to do this:

1. Soulful Education is about relating to students as souls. My love stems from my awareness of each student's infinite worth and potential.

2. It is essential to love our students unconditionally. The teacher-student relationship should not depend on how much the student is intellectually successful, likable, or well-behaved.

a. It is essential to love *all* of our students. There will always be challenging students who disrupt the class and throw me off track. That student is still worthy of loving.

b. It is especially important to relate personally to the students on the margins—the quiet students who tend to disappear in the classroom.

As we've established, it can be scary to care about our students. Loving always brings vulnerability along with it. Students come and go; we can be forgotten, disappointed, and even hurt by our willingness to care. But there is no other way. At the end of the day, I have to remind myself that teaching—this holy profession—is not about me. It is about how I serve others. My students, as strong and independent as they seem, are in great need of my nourishment and support. Soulful Education obligates us to be there for them, for all of them.

How can I do this? How is it possible to love my students unconditionally? It really depends on how I look at them. Throughout my time in primary school, at university, and then as an adult in yeshiva, I felt that most of my educators looked at me only through the scope and content of their class. My history teacher cared about me on Mondays and Wednesdays, 9:30–10:30 a.m.; my Bible teacher, 2:00–4:00 p.m. on Tuesday and Thursday afternoons during the semester that I

Mentoring from love allows the students to dare and to grow.

was in his class. Other than that, I may have received a nod in the hallway or the standard, passing, two-minute "How are you?" conversation.

I asked my own kids, "Who in your school do you think really cares about you?" They all gave me the same answer: "Moshe, the janitor. He always smiles and gives us candy." Good for Moshe, but what an incredible indictment of an educational institution. The school is so focused on content and books that they forget they are teaching human beings.

Soulful Education demands a paradigm shift in how we relate to our students. First of all, we're shifting our idea of the *scope* of the student-teacher relationship. My investment is not limited to the time and topic of the class. My student is not just a receptacle into which I pour knowledge. The student is created in the image of God and has a unique soul. I need to relate to my students as souls, with infinite worth and infinite potential.

Often our students are fragile and insecure. If my students are high schoolers, they are in the process of growing up and cannot be expected to be fully mature and responsible people. As a friend of mine says, "'Teenage' and 'stupid' are synonyms." They are discovering themselves, often comparing themselves to others and coming out on the short end.

It is our responsibility to see the bigger picture, to see them not just as students in our classes, but as young people on life journeys. Leadership expert Sharon Daloz-Parks writes that a mentor does not see the student where he or she is now, but senses the inner worth of a student and his or her potential.[16] The mentor recognizes the greatness in a student, even when the student can see only his or her shortcomings and mess-ups.

When the mentor sees the greater potential in the student, it is as if he or she is holding up a mirror,

> At the end of the day, I have to remind myself that teaching—this holy profession—is not about me. It is about how I serve others. My students, as strong and independent as they seem, are in great need of my nourishment and support.

showing the student the better self who is already there, but that he or she cannot yet see. Glimpsing this better self, the student is encouraged, inspired, and motivated to become that better self. This is true Soulful Education: taking a holistic view of the student—seeing the student's past, present, and future all at the same time.

Mentoring from love allows the students to dare and to grow. Their future better selves are calling to them, but their present fearful selves are saying, "It's risky to try something new; I might not excel. I might fail. What will people say?" If we do not encourage our students to take new steps, to venture out into their life journey, and offer them the love and support they need, then we are preparing them for a life of hesitation and regret over not having dared to move forward.

When Does the Love Begin?

My love for my students does not begin when I walk into the classroom, when I meet them for the first time. My love for my students starts from the very first moment of my preparation for the class and continues long after the class is over. Loving students is an attitude that can work only if it suffuses the entire teaching process.

> Loving students is an attitude that can work only if it suffuses the entire teaching process.

A friend of mine loves to invite guests for meals. The food he cooks is something indescribably special. I once asked him what special spices he used. He smiled at me and said, "It's not the spice, the ingredients, or the recipes. It's that I am thinking about my guests, thinking about giving them pleasure, from the moment that I invite them—while I am planning the menu, buying the food, chopping, stirring, and cooking. It's the love that gives the taste."

At first, I thought my friend was a bit wacko. Really? Love gives the taste? Now, I know that he understood something extremely profound.

When I learn for myself, my focus is to master the texts and to go as deeply as I can. But when I learn material in order to teach it, I have a very different mind-set. The goal is not for *me* to understand; the goal is for my *students* to understand. When love imbues the preparation, the process ceases to be a burden and becomes an act of giving and generosity. My preparation acquires a different flavor that tangibly impacts the classroom experience.

In short, Soulful Education demands me to feel love for my students, even from the moment of preparation.

It is challenging to love our students. There are moments when a student can seem like an enemy, wearing us down, making us want to go home and cry. When my oldest daughter decided to go into education, I said to her, "I'm giving you all of my wisdom in three words: 'Love those monsters.'"

There are moments in our teaching lives when we feel like we can't take it anymore, when our entire self-image plummets into an endless abyss. These are precisely the moments to remind ourselves of Soulful Education's message: "It's not about me. Let go of the ego voice. Deep breath. Something is not working. What do *they* need now?"

A Lasting Love

Although classes provide a regular framework for cultivating a relationship, loving students does not end when the class is over. The class is the stepping-stone for what happens in life, and the real goal of teaching is not just the class but also what happens in one, two, or five years. Classroom interactions can ignite a relationship that lasts for years. I have students who still contact me twenty years after we first learned together. We have all forgotten everything we learned in that classroom, but the relationship forged there provides support for a lifetime. Although I was probably the least knowledgeable teacher on the staff, my students knew that I cared about them for who they were, not just for how they performed, and that has made all the difference.

Listening Means Loving

How is caring for students expressed? By listening to them.

A few years ago, I had the opportunity to guest-teach at a high school. I sat in on a twelfth-grade class and opened by asking them, "When does anyone on the staff openly listen to you?" They looked at me in silence, a bit bewildered. Then, in one voice they all answered, "Never. No one." At the end of their four years—the most formative years of their lives—they had not found a single teacher who patiently listened to them.

I had met their teacher, an extremely warm and caring individual. He had left a successful law career to go into teaching solely because he was idealistic and wanted to contribute to education. He would have claimed unequivocally that he loves his students. Yet this love and caring had not translated into listening.

In Soulful Education there is a simple question that connects caring for students with listening: "Is there anything more you would like to add?" It is a question that reflects the willingness to simply be there for the other person.

Several years ago I taught at a large Jewish retreat in England; there were over two thousand participants. We were housed in a university that was empty for winter break. The first morning I rose early and went down to the massive university cafeteria that seated over a thousand people. There were only a dozen or so early risers who had already arrived. I took my breakfast to a far corner and looked forward to some quiet time before the rush of the crowds and the hectic teaching day began.

Just as I got settled, to my surprise, another early riser came over and sat down right next to me. As I began my first mouthful of breakfast, this total stranger turned to me, poked me in the shoulder, and said, "Do you know what love is?"

I thought to myself, isn't it a bit early for love? My less gracious side growled, "A giant, empty cafeteria and just my luck—he sits down next to *me*!"

"No," I replied. "Please enlighten me."

"Love," he said, poking me once more, "is curiosity." "Oy," I said to myself. That was not what I was expecting. Now he had my attention. "What do you mean, curiosity?"

"When you love someone, you want to learn everything about them. You stay up all night talking. You ask questions and can listen endlessly. When you don't love someone, you're always looking for ways to end the conversation. Listening and loving go together." And with that he got up and left, leaving me open-mouthed—and oblivious to my breakfast.

A few years ago a veteran teacher told me that he wanted to become a better listener. He asked me how he could learn to do that. I said to him, "To become a better listener, work on loving people more. As you love more, you will naturally discover how easy it is to listen." This truism of the connection between love and curiosity is tested in the patience of an educator, inviting him or her to listen without judgment or edginess. The effect of this listening is to encourage and enable the students to listen to themselves deeply.

Who Is Teaching Whom?

I once had a "student from hell." Every time she saw me in the hallway, she would run up and ask me a question. A difficult, eclectic question that I had no idea how to answer. Before I could even begin to respond, she would then rattle off another question. While I was balancing these two questions, she would then ask, "Is it okay if I ask you another question?" Within thirty seconds I was exhausted, blitzed by questions, clueless how to respond.

I began to avoid her in the halls. Peeking out from the classroom to see if the coast was clear, I would race to the faculty lounge. I felt like a coward and an educational failure, but on the other hand, I just didn't have the emotional resources to continually handle the onslaught of questions. I felt drained and weary.

It took me way too long to realize that this student was not really interested in the answers. She was lonely, socially awkward, and didn't know how to begin a conversation. Since I was the teacher, she struck up the conversation with questions.

I eventually realized that my relationship with this student was not at all by chance. After months of lamenting these demanding and draining interactions, I finally understood. I needed to learn something that only she could teach me. It was not by chance that she accosted me with her questions. I needed to experience this student. This student was not a student from hell but a student from heaven. In fact, this student was not my student at all, but rather my teacher. She had come into my life to teach me something about myself.

> To become a better listener, work on loving people more. As you love more, you will naturally discover how easy it is to listen.

I had thought that I was a caring person and teacher. I had thought that I was empathetic and a good listener. But apparently my heart was not big enough to include her. I needed to be stretched, to grow in my caring. A physical trainer knows that to get into better shape we need to get to our limit and then push a little bit more. So too with emotions. I had reached a comfort zone of relating to students. My heart was big enough to include most of them, but not all of them. This challenging student was, unknowingly, my "love trainer," forcing me to stretch my heart when I thought I was at my limit. Apparently my loving muscles needed to be stretched, to find space to care about her too. After reframing how I looked at her, I began to look forward to the difficult questions after class, excited by the opportunity not to run away but to engage this student in the way that she needed.

Rav Kook writes that the primary purpose of learning Torah is to clear away the obstacles preventing us from being loving human beings.[17] The Talmud scholar should be the most loving person in the community. It's not about *the amount* of knowledge that the scholar has but rather *the effect* of the knowledge. That knowledge should enable someone to become a vessel of godliness, a compassionate and loving human being.

Loving the Students on the Margins

I doubt that any experienced teacher would openly profess to favoring one student over another. When asked, we all quickly declare that we care equally about all of our students, just as we care equally about all our children. Nevertheless, in content-focused settings where the goals of the class are discrete and quantifiable, the more intellectually gifted students naturally gain center stage, while the less gifted or attentive students drift to the margins.

I once experienced an extreme example of this phenomenon while visiting my son's high school Talmud class. I soon realized that the teacher was teaching to the five smartest and most actively engaged students, while twenty other students fiddled and daydreamed. When I related the incident to the principal, he replied, "Yes, we like the bookish ones ..."

There will always be students who are reluctant to jump into the center of a class discussion; students who rarely, if ever, raise their hands in class. They are easy to ignore. It is easy for the teacher to assume that everything is okay with them.

Recently a teacher shared with me how happy she was with her class. She said, "The students were into it; we had a great discussion." I asked her what percentage of the students actively participated in the class. She said about half of them, maybe even more. Then I asked her about the students who did not say anything. "Do you think the students who did not contribute to the conversation had nothing to say?" "No," she replied. "Of course they had something, but ..."

Soulful Education stresses safe space and would never push a student who does not want to talk in class to share. But we have to acknowledge that this quiet student also has a voice. And this voice needs to be heard—if not for the sake of the class, then for the sake of the student.

It is incumbent on the soulful teacher to become aware of the quiet students, not to let them drift away or assume everything is okay just because they are not causing any problems. I have used several methods for enabling these students to hear their voices:

1. **Pairing:** Build sharing in pairs into the class structure more often. The quiet students may be reluctant to be the center of attention but may be more open to sharing with another student, which is less overwhelming.

2. **Alternative media:** Students express themselves in different ways. It could be that a student does not want to comment aloud but would eagerly share insights through writing, drawing, or drama.

3. **After class:** It may be necessary to set a time after class to hear the voice of these students. It could be that they will only open up when alone with their teacher. The teacher needs to be proactive in enabling these students to discover and hear their own voices.

Part 2

The Six Essential Steps of Soulful Education

Bringing Soulfulness into Everything You Teach

When the aim of our teaching is an interesting classroom experience, our focus is on mindful engagement. The objective is to teach ideas, information, and skills as efficiently and effectively as possible.

But when the aim is to make a long-term impact beyond the classroom, the experience within the classroom requires a process, a choreographed progression. From our experience at Ayeka, the road map that leads to a long-term impact includes six essential steps:

1. Transitioning into the class

2. Introducing the learning

3. Mindful engagement

4. Heartful engagement

5. Summarizing the learning

6. Transitioning out of the class

I often compare this six-step process to inviting guests to a meal, in which the teacher is the host and the students are the guests. When honored guests come to a feast, you don't move straight into the main course; you want to create a full experience, beginning with the excitement of welcoming them into your space and building up to the crescendo of the main dish, making sure they feel well taken care of as they depart, and giving them plenty of "food for thought" as they return to their lives.

I believe that this is a close parallel for the steps that must take place in a classroom for the experience to be fulfilling and to have a lasting effect on the student:

1. Welcoming the guests—transitioning into the class

2. Appetizers—introducing the learning

3. First course—mindful engagement

4. Main course—heartful engagement

5. Dessert—summarizing the learning

6. Escorting the guests—transitioning out of the class

I will go more deeply into each of these steps in the pages that follow.

Transitioning into the Class

Just because they are there—doesn't mean they are there.
We cannot multi-task the soul.

We live in an obsessively multi-tasking world. Linda Stone of Microsoft coined the expression for our time: "continuous partial attention." We have grown accustomed to juggling a number of tasks at once, never fully devoting ourselves to a single one.

It is very rare for someone to be fully present and focused on one task. I often ask students at the beginning of a class, "On a 1 to 10 scale of being fully present, what number would you give yourselves right now?" The typical response is 5 or 6.

If my goal is only to convey information, then it is not a calamity if the students are only borderline present. They can grasp the ideas; they can give the class 50 percent of their attention and still probably ace the test. We know that even when we only partially listen to a conversation, we are still able to recall the main points.

But we cannot multi-task our souls. We will never be deeply impacted by any idea if we are only partially engaged. If we are not fully invested in the task, if in addition to our minds, our hearts and souls are not fully focused on the moment, there is no chance for the experience to be transformative.

The Problem of Multi-tasking
A Psychological Perspective

I believe that multi-tasking is one of the most defining and troubling phenomena of the modern era. Technologies designed to make us more productive are also making us scattered, fueling our natural psychological reluctance to fully engage.

Rav Shagar writes:

> The challenge of focusing on something fully and for an extended period of time stems from this—it is difficult to shrink oneself and say: "I am certain that this is what I should be doing," and [it is easier to] continually allow oneself to live in the vast spiritual/existential world of possibilities.[1]

Focusing fully on one activity is a decision that requires a commitment, a willingness to wear blinders that divert my attention from anything else. In fact, the word "decision" itself is connected linguistically to "incision," cutting off. When we pursue one endeavor, we cut off all other choices and paths. We obligate ourselves to fulfilling one and only one goal. Like an incision, the decision to focus can be a painful process.

Rav Shagar empathizes with the challenge of focusing on one activity:

> The human being lives always with a sense of running out of time. It is difficult to contract endless possibilities. There is a sweetness in allowing for boundless potential. There is never a perfect choice. There is an inner fear and trembling over choosing one option and having to live with that choice. It is always preferable to "sit on the fence," preserving an abundance of opportunities.
>
> The drive to multi-task is not erroneous or in itself invalid. The (psychological) problem emerges when we are addicted to multi-tasking, and this drive begins to control us. When we cannot desist from multi-tasking.[2]

As opposed to focusing, multi-tasking allows us to engage, at least partially, in an undertaking without cutting off other possibilities. I don't have to make a decision; I can leave all of my possibilities open. This is similar to the fear of commitment that we see in skittish brides and grooms and first-time home buyers, but drawn down to a much smaller but more pervasive scale. Multi-tasking can become addictive, imbuing our lives, every time we begin to focus on any one thing, with the real fear that we are missing something else, something potentially more important. Almost anyone with a smartphone is affected by this on some annoying level, and for too many it becomes a block to serious thought and long-term-oriented action.

One of the main reasons why multi-tasking is so tempting is because it is much less risky than making a decision. When I commit to a single goal, I run the risk of making the wrong choice, of failing. When I multi-task, I don't put myself on the line for any single goal; I am not "all in." In the words of Rav Shagar, I do not have to shrink myself; I can engage in one activity while still living in the vast world of possibilities.

Our students sense the risk of failure from the earliest ages. They wear multi-tasking like a shield, protecting themselves from the possible humiliation of losing or failing. They carry with them the built-in excuse of not having been "all in" on any endeavor. For soulful educators, breaking this multi-tasking shield—that is, inviting students to lay it down—is the first step in allowing them to fully engage and become affected by what goes on in the classroom.

A Spiritual Perspective

Rav Abraham Isaac Kook writes that multi-tasking is a form of spiritual infidelity:

> One needs to seek God in the midst of what one is doing. When praying—then seek God in understanding and proper spiritual focus of the prayers. And do not stray to think about other things, since when one is involved in service, God dwells precisely in this service, and there he will find God and not elsewhere.
>
> And when one is involved in Torah, he should know that he will find God when he studies well, and through this he will find God, because at that moment God is revealed through this service.
>
> And when he is involved in doing acts of kindness (*chesed*), then he should seek God only regarding how to improve his *chesed*. And so in everything that he does, as truly there is nothing in this world that is not for His honor. Therefore everything he does—everything should be for His command and His will ... when he strives with his mind and energy to do everything as well as he can, and then it will come out that he "knows" God, in all of his ways.

> When a person is fully engaged, whether in thought or action, he should become happy in what he is doing and not chase after something else, as the entire world devolves precisely into that single moment.[3]

For Rav Kook, committing to a single activity does not shrink my options or narrow my interaction with my surroundings; rather, the opposite. When I focus intently, committing all of my intellectual, emotional, and physical powers to one action, I drill down so deeply that I touch the entire world. I discover the infinite through the finite, the eternal through the momentary, the universal through the particular. When I touch and fully embrace what I am doing, infinity and eternity are present in each moment. At that moment, I know God.

> For soulful educators, breaking this multi-tasking shield—that is, inviting students to lay it down—is the first step in allowing them to fully engage and become affected by what goes on in the classroom.

In contrast, when I am unable to commit to one action, I am demonstrating my spiritual uncertainty. Multi-tasking reflects my doubts regarding surrendering to a relationship. Inside, my voice is whispering, "Are you completely sure about this? Are you definitely 100 percent convinced that this is the best option for you at this moment?" The answer I almost always give is, "I'm pretty sure, but not 100 percent." So I engage in other things at the same time. The consequence is that spiritual growth becomes impossible. I cannot deepen a relationship that I am not committed to 100 percent.

I could never have a soulful conversation with another person while multi-tasking. And how much more so does this apply to my soulful conversations with God. If I am unwilling to give myself over to prayer or thought, even for a short period of time, how can I expect to develop my relationship with God? To move from shallow to deep, and from deep to deeper? And since I myself am created in the image of God, does my inability to deepen my relationship with God ultimately lead to an inability to deepen my relationship with myself?

The Talmud was well aware of the slippery slope of multi-tasking. In *Sukkah* 25a, the Talmud rules, "One who is involved in a mitzvah is exempt from another mitzvah." This isn't intuitively obvious; the Talmud has an interest in increasing the number of mitzvot performed on earth, so isn't it a good idea for each of us to engage in as many as possible, all the time? Yet the Talmud understands that mitzvah multi-tasking defeats the purpose. Scattered performance of multiple mitzvot is not better than focused performance of just one. Doing more, in this case, is actually doing less.

Rav Kook writes that being fully invested in a particular action leads to a sense of gratitude for the moment. Every moment has something within it that is a gift from above. It is for us to discern what is being given, whether a particular blessing, challenge, or simply life itself. Our gratitude for this moment eventually, with practice and intention, leads to love for the giver of this moment, namely the Creator of the universe.

> For us as soulful educators, helping our students transition from their multi-tasking world to a universe of full engagement, focus, and commitment is one of the greatest gifts that we can give them.

Full intention, gratitude, and love are intrinsically linked, according to Rav Kook. Multi-tasking is the obstacle precluding advancing to deeper gratitude and love. For us as soulful educators, helping our students transition from their multi-tasking world to a universe of full engagement, focus, and commitment is one of the greatest gifts that we can give them, setting them on a path through which they can begin to hear the spiritual voices within themselves.

Setting the Transition—For Students

So our challenge is, in today's multi-tasking world, how can we bring our students to be more fully present in our teaching? If not a 10 on our scale, then at least a 9. Is this doable? And if not, are we resigned to our teaching having only a minimal impact?

For way too many years, I made the mistake of entering a classroom and jumping straight into the learning. I loved the material so much that I couldn't wait to get into it and bring it to the students. I was bursting with excitement. I was also oblivious to reality. The students did not walk into the classroom with the same mind-set. I offered no transition, no opportunity for them to become more present.

Step 1 in our educational road map is transition: transitioning from the "before-class" life to becoming present in the class.

Judaism is very big on transitions that increase our awareness of what we are about to do:

- Before the climax in prayer, the silent standing prayer (*Amidah*), we take three steps backward and then three steps forward.
- Before lighting candles on Friday night, we circle our hands three times and then cover our eyes.
- Before eating we recite blessings. And before reciting blessings, many people have a custom to say a phrase about uniting with the presence of God.

Before teaching, we need to enable our students to transition into our classroom and become more present and focused.

Soulful Education does not require a lot of time to do this. We need to get to the main course of teaching. But how we welcome our guests will influence the quality of the whole experience. This transition period:

- Should take up only the first three to five minutes of a class.
- Should have everyone active.
- Should be enjoyable and not make anyone uncomfortable.

I often ask students to turn to the person next to them and simply share what is holding them back from being more present in the class. What is occupying them now, and what do they need to let go? Each person talks for one minute, acknowledging and focusing directly on the issue that is presently distracting. This activity forces everyone to be active—talking and then listening—and takes up only two to three minutes of class time. I don't want to turn this transitional phase into a class discussion, which runs the risk of either taking too much time or enabling one person to potentially dominate the moment. Everyone needs to be active, and everyone needs to open their mouth, but I want to limit the amount of time this transition consumes.

Alternative transition ideas:

- Do a short stretching exercise with the class.
- Ask everyone to take three deep breaths and relax.
- Ask a question to the class that builds in short answers. For example: "What word comes up for you when I say …?"

Short. Active. Enjoyable. Comfortable.

Making the Transition—For Teachers

We have said that the most important moment for the student occurs *after* the class is over. But the most important moment for the teacher occurs *before* the class begins. Just like my students, I too need to transition to full focus.

I have been shocked by how many educators have told me that they are marginally focused in class. They admit to being distracted by the many other tasks they have to accomplish. Often something happens right before class that occupies their attention, or they have an important engagement right after class. They multi-task their teaching.

Our students will never be more present than we are. So the question posed to our students is equally relevant to us: in today's multi-tasking world, how can we, the educators, bring ourselves to be more fully present in our teaching?

> The most important moment for the teacher occurs *before* the class begins.

I consider the moment before actually walking into the classroom to be the most important moment for my teaching. How do I transition into the teaching setting? Do I just barge into the room, mind racing from my previous engagement? Do I acknowledge that I am moving into a potentially sacred moment? Do I pause to gather and center myself?

Before walking into the classroom, I stop for a few seconds to gather my thoughts and direct my focus for the next round of teaching. It would be wonderful to take ten or even five minutes to reflect on what I am about to do and to fully compose myself. The exigencies of my schedule usually don't allow me to pause for more than about twenty seconds.

> Our students will never be more present than we are.

Years ago, I composed this short saying to help me transition into the moment: "Please, God, give me the will and wisdom to best serve my students." When I say it slowly, it takes only ten seconds. If I pause before and after saying it, perhaps twenty seconds total. But the effect of concentrating on these words is powerful. I let go of the mess and turbulence filling my head and begin to devote myself to my students.

I strongly recommend that teachers compose a short mantra they can recite before entering their classes. It should be something that forces them to stop, focus, and transition safely into their teaching.

Short. Focused. Personal. Centering.

Staying in the Zone

Not only do I recite my short mantra before beginning to teach but I also often return to it during my teaching. Many times during a class I can be thrown off my center, distracted either by something happening in the class or by confusion and turmoil in my head.

When I've asked teachers, "What throws you off your zone while teaching?" their answers seem to be never-ending:

- An annoying student
- A bored look on a student's face
- Remembering my to-do list
- The air-conditioning stopped working
- A sneeze
- Someone knocked on the door
- My shoelace came undone
- Recalling a previous conversation

- Making a blooper or a Freudian slip
- Figuring out how many days are left in the school year

When we are thrown off our zone, it is normal to need a moment to re-transition into becoming focused and present again in the class. What matters isn't the amount of time, but that those moments are taken consciously, with intentionality. This transitioning period is critical. The whole learning experience depends on the transition going smoothly and successfully.

I remember a few occasions when my family hosted meals and invested so much in preparation—shopping, cooking, cleaning, setting the table—that by the time the guests arrived, we would be exhausted and even resentful of them coming. We opened the door and greeted them with bothered, languid faces. Needless to say, the whole hosting experience was doomed from that moment forward.

Transitioning from life into the teaching-learning moment requires full acknowledgment and intentionality.

Introducing the Learning

Ayeka—where are *you*—in this subject?
Pluck your soul string.

After transitioning, we are still not ready to actually begin learning. First, the teacher needs to personally introduce or frame the learning.

When we walk into a classroom, we naturally begin to engage from the shoulders up. We go into thinking mode. We want to be smart, to ask good questions, to use long words. We have been conditioned from an early age to view the classroom as the site of exclusively intellectual inter-action. It is not a place for emotional, spiritual, or personal engagement. Honor and recognition go to the one who excels intellectually.

To break out of this ingrained mentality, the teacher needs to model his or her own personal engagement with the subject. This does not need to take a lot of time. As discussed earlier, modeling how to "pluck our soul string" using harmonic vibrations may take only five or six minutes. But it is essential to break out of engaging primarily or exclusively with our minds if we want our learning to impact our lives. For our students, we must consciously demonstrate that we are personally involved with the topic.

This is a huge paradigm shift for teachers. Modeling involves openness, vulnerability, sincerity, and acknowledging that I am a work-in-progress who also needs and wants to grow through learning. It is, unsurprisingly, very challenging to model personal engagement.

I often feel a moment of awkwardness and hesitation just before I begin to personally frame the learning. Questions race through my head: "Will my students mock me? Will I cross the line and share too much? Am I crazy to be doing this when all the other teachers are just focusing on the texts?"

What has helped me take this leap and model vulnerability is to constantly remind myself that I am here to provide a service to my students. It is not about me; it is about them. What do they need? My goal as a teacher is to enable the students to bring their learning into their lives after the class is over. I am here not because I love the subject matter or because as a kid I liked school. I am here not because I love to study. I am here to help and mentor my students—whatever it takes. If I want my students to be brave, to confront their work-in-progress-ness, and to take the next steps in their lives, then I need to step out of my formal teaching mode and become

> **For our students, we must consciously demonstrate that we are personally involved with the topic.**

a real human being for them for a few minutes. How? By overcoming my insecurities, taking a deep breath, and jumping in. I need to be open and truthful in front of them.

I recently asked a group of veteran educators what would be different about their teaching if they could let go of their fears and insecurities in the classroom. If I could offer them a magic potion of courage and emancipate them from what makes them anxious in their classes, what would be different about their teaching?

They responded:

- They would be happier in their teaching.
- Their smile and laugh would be bigger.
- They would be more open to questions.
- They would be more spontaneous.
- They would work less hard to play the role of the teacher and more be themselves.
- They would be more likely to say, "I don't know."
- They would flow with the pace of the class and take more risks.
- They would risk getting "off-script."
- They would love their students for who they are, and not as "hallmarks" of their success as a teacher.

What holds these teachers back from letting go of their classroom fears and anxiety?

- Their concerns over how they may appear in their students' eyes
- Their worry over their lack of knowledge
- Their need for control
- Their need to be admired

Step 2, framing the learning, is an opportunity for the teacher to be whole-heartedly in the classroom. In her TED Talk in Houston, Texas, in 2010, vulnerability researcher Brené Brown insightfully pointed out that the word "courage" stems from the French word *coeur*, which means "heart." Someone who is courageous is someone who brings wholeheartedness into his or her life. Framing the learning, our "appetizer," sets the mood for the rest of the learning and prepares students to open not only their minds but also and especially their hearts.

Framing the learning is an opportunity for the teacher to be wholeheartedly in the classroom.

Step 3

Mindful Engagement

Jewish wisdom is more than information.

Step 3 is the actual learning section of the class. This is when the teacher introduces new material and ideas through study, lecture, and discussion, often in a mind-to-mind fashion.

Soulful Education adds one wrinkle to this part of the learning experience. We want to make sure that the mind-to-mind learning is also *mindful*. That is to say, while focusing my mind on an issue, I have not disconnected my mind from my life. While learning the subject matter, I am also aware of what the subject matter means to me. I am not using *a* mind, but *my* mind. This means that while I seek to understand the content, I am also open to my relationship with the content.

Henri Nouwen, professor at the Harvard Graduate School of Divinity, writes about how to learn a holy text:

> Spiritual reading means not simply reading about spiritual things but also reading about spiritual things in a spiritual way. We can become very knowledgeable about spiritual matters without becoming truly spiritual people.
>
> Spiritual reading is far from easy in our modern, intellectual world, where we tend to make everything we read subject to analysis and discussion. Instead of wondering if we agree or disagree with what we have read, we should wonder which words are spoken directly to us and connect directly with our most personal story. Instead of thinking about the words as potential subjects for an interesting dialogue or paper, we should be willing to let them penetrate into the most hidden corners of our heart.

> There is a form of listening in which we keep wondering which words are written for us, for our own spiritual journey. Spiritual reading is a way of reading the word with our whole being, our present condition, our past experiences, and our future aspirations.
>
> As we slowly let the written words enter into our minds and descend into our hearts, we become different people.[4]

For me, the key word in his writing is in the last sentence: "slowly." Often, in a mind-to-mind approach to learning, we are racing to comprehension. Who can know it faster? Those who read and understand quickly are given honor. Henri Nouwen teaches us how to use our minds soulfully, how not to divorce our thinking from the rest of our being. He changes the question from "Did you understand the material?" to "How does your understanding of the material affect you?"

> **Education should be not only mastering data but also using the information to advance our personal clarity, to grow and deepen ourselves.**

This question subtly changes our attitude to the subject matter. It is no longer dry information. The content of what we are learning now becomes a form of guidance that we want to integrate into our lives. Education should be not only mastering data but also using the information to advance our personal clarity, to grow and deepen ourselves. The ceaseless pursuit of disconnected data can lead to an intellectual and education malaise, a sense of ennui, begging the question: What is the point of all these facts, ideas, and concepts?

When I teach, I often ask my students to imagine they are seeing the texts for the very first time. If they have encountered these texts before, I don't want them to rely on the theories that they came up with the last time they encountered the texts. That is too easy and will prevent them from letting themselves jump in now, to be affected. Previous understandings may have been appropriate for who they were then, but now they are different, and they should give themselves the opportunity to see everything with new eyes.

Step 4

Heartful Engagement

Any learning, without processing, never happened.
Learn—Process—Share
Learning = accessing + harmonizing the three voices of the soul

Rav Kook writes:

> In the education of an individual, and so too with the education
> of the collective, the nation and all of humanity, we need to pay
> special attention to spiritual unity. That is—that the intellect will
> directly shape the emotions, and emotion will shape the imagina-
> tion, and the imaginative powers will influence one's actions.
>
> Because when there is a breakdown between these elements—
> then destruction finds a place to dwell.[5]

Rav Kook's words were a shock for me. Actually three shocks:

- "Spiritual unity." The goal of education is spiritual unity. Not comprehension, analysis, or innovation?
- "Imagination." Imagination? What could be the imagination's role in
  education?
- "Then destruction finds a place to dwell." If we do not foster spiritual unity, then we may actually be creating harm?

The goal of education is spiritual unity. We are spiritual beings; education is the tool for clarifying and deepening our spiritual selves. Our intellectual, emotional, and active sides are all essential. But when education
becomes skewed to one side or the other, the resulting imbalance creates a
disintegrated and, consequently, unhealthy human being.

According to the Kabbalah, there are three primary voices of the soul: the mind (*neshamah*), the heart (*ruach*), and the body (*nefesh*).[6] The soul utilizes these channels to speak to us in different and distinct ways. Spiritual unity involves accessing and harmonizing these three voices of the soul. All educational engagement needs to balance these three human qualities. We don't want to divide our existence by the intellectual, emotional, and physical components. The mind, heart, and body need to work in unison and harmony.

Step 4, heartful engagement, is when we begin to process and personalize what we learned in step 3.

It is sad but unfortunately true that learning, without processing, never happened. I have forgotten countless classes that I attended. I have even forgotten countless courses that I have taught! This is not just a product of aging but also the result of neglect, the failure to bring the content into my heart and to personalize it. While I have forgotten closets' worth of ideas, whatever became personally meaningful for me has not disappeared.

Almost two thousand years ago, the Talmud noted, "A person learns only where his heart is engaged" (*Avodah Zarah* 19a). How can we bring learning from our minds to our hearts?

First of all, we have to recognize that the heart learns differently than the mind.[7] The mind grasps ideas in a moment and is ready to move on. We've all had moments in the classroom when we've said to ourselves, "Okay, I got it. Let's keep moving." The mind wants more—new—faster. We groan when a teacher belabors a point. Reviewing material can be painful. Sometimes it takes only a moment for our impatience to kick in. Once our brain absorbs an idea, we feel there is no reason to dwell on it. When the goal is purely intellectual, we can move at lightning speed and feel a powerful resistance to slowing down. The mind is interested in more data and does not pause to integrate or connect the ideas with our lives. The mind is on its own journey, often accompanied by disconnection.

> **The heart learns differently than the mind.**

But the heart, the connective tissue within us, learns slowly. I need time to reflect, ruminate, and wonder how the content affects me, at this moment in my life.

The heartful learning piece of Soulful Education blends Rav Kook's three elements—emotion, imagination, and action—with the intellect. Step 4 involves:

- Being alone
- Reflecting on how to personalize my learning
- Creating something physical
- Using my imagination
- Talking from the heart

Step 4 moves from "What do the sources say?" to "What do the sources say—to me?"

Engaging Through Personal Writing

For me, the most comfortable way to engage in this process is to ask my students to respond to four questions in writing. I instruct them to write for just three to five minutes, in silence, to help everyone focus fully.

To ease people into this new process, it is important to set several rules:

- **No competing.** We don't share what we write with the group. This alleviates a lot of anxiety, eliminates the tendency to compare ourselves to others, and allows for greater honesty and openness.
- **No self-judgment.** Whatever emerges is fine. Don't be self-critical. Don't say to yourself that you are not deep, eloquent, and creative. Don't criticize your word choices or grammar. We do not have to be writers to do this exercise. This is an opportunity to check in with ourselves.
- **No self-censoring. No editing.** We need to let ourselves be guided by our sense of intuition and try to write in a stream-of-consciousness mode.

During these few moments of writing, the whole tenor of the class changes dramatically. The atmosphere becomes thick as everyone's seriousness and focus fill the room. Faces are down, close to the paper and laptop screens. Pens held intensely, fingers tapping furiously.

Why do I love this method for introducing heartful engagement? First, everyone is active at the same time! Everyone is engaged! It is unusual in a classroom setting for everyone to be active. Usually one person talks and others listen. Even if the class is divided into small groups, there are always some people speaking and others listening. But during a writing exercise, everyone is active.

Second, the students are alone in their own space. Astonishingly, in education today, students are rarely left to experience learning alone. Mainstream, accepted educational settings include lecture, small-group discussion, or partnered learning. But the individual student is almost never given alone time in class for personal processing. I often ask myself, "How on earth can we hope our students will authentically personalize the content of our teaching when we never give them the opportunity to be alone with it? When will they have the chance to hear their own voice?"

> I often ask myself, "How on earth can we hope our students will authentically personalize the content of our teaching when we never give them the opportunity to be alone with it?"

Each student is his or her own unique reality. The Midrash audaciously observes that at the Mount Sinai revelation, "everyone heard a different voice of God."[8] Every human being has to blend the learning into his or her own life. There is a lot going on in the inner lives of our students, but without reflective time it is almost impossible for them to access it. As our students experience formal education, they spend most of their time listening to others. When can they make the learning their own?

In this fourth step, students are given time alone together with a prompt that helps them focus on how their learning connects to their own lives. Writing is a great focusing tool. It ensures that students are not just thinking or talking about how to personalize their learning. They are also physically entering a creative production process (writing), which forces them to more fully confront exactly where they are vis-à-vis the subject matter.

The writing exercise is based on four questions:

1. The first question is always neutral: "Where are you (*Ayeka?*) regarding the subject we studied? How would you describe your relationship to the ideas we learned together?"

2. The second question is futuristic: "How do you think these ideas can affect your life? If you were to become more connected to these ideas, what do you think would be different in your life?"

3. The third question reflects the gap between the present reality and the future possibility: "What do you think are the obstacles for you to reach this future reality? What is holding you back?"

4. The fourth question leads into visualizing life after class: "If you could give yourself one small but practical piece of advice to help you grow, something that you could actually implement in the upcoming week or month—based on what we learned and what you wrote—what piece of advice would you give yourself?"

This is an easy template to implement in teaching. It is applicable to all subjects. The teacher simply needs to extract the primary idea, value, or behavior that the students should grapple with and insert it into the writing exercise.

For example, let's say a class is studying history. Based on the content and students' personalities, the teacher will decide which idea is most salient and relevant. It might be leadership, political activism, bravery, dedication, civil rights, idealism, or honesty. The template would then work like this:

1. On a scale of 1 to 10, how would you describe yourself vis-à-vis the value of leadership? Write a few sentences to explain why you chose that number.

2. What would be different about your life if you could magically rise up a couple of notches on this scale?

3. What do you think is holding you back from being more of a leader?

4. What small but practical piece of advice would you give yourself to help take the first step toward becoming more of a leader?

Any chapter of the Torah, any section of the Mishnah or Talmud, any aspect of ethics or Jewish law does well with this template. Recently a teacher I know told me about how he applied this model to his prayer class:

1. On a scale of 1 to 10, how would you describe yourself vis-à-vis your relationship with prayer? Write a few sentences about why you chose that number.

2. What would be different about your life if you could magically rise up a few notches on this scale?

3. What do you think is holding you back from having a deeper prayer experience?

4. What small but practical piece of advice would you give yourself to help you take the first step toward building a more fulfilling prayer life?

The most important question is question 2, and this is also the question that invokes Rav Kook's emphasis on imagination. Considering "How would your life be different if ..." propels us toward the future. We are invited to envision new selves. We are not asked to commit to dramatic and life-altering resolutions, but we are contemplating small steps to bring what we are learning into our lives.

Imagination is our power to envision a reality that does not exist yet. My better self does not presently exist in reality; it exists only in my imagination. By imagining and envisioning our better selves, we are already moving toward a new and better future. For me to become my best self, I first need to imagine a better version of myself and then reflect on what is holding me back from getting there. This is the goal of the writing exercise.

Soulful Education is always future based:

- Imagining a better self
- Aiming for the learning to have an impact *after* the class
- Aiming for the learning to help rebuild the Garden of Eden

Rav Kook writes that unlike all other cultures, the Jewish People is not a product of its past but of its future. All other cultures celebrate and find their distinctiveness from their past history. Their present is a function of their past. For the Jewish People, however, the present is a function of the future.

We behave in the present because we want to reach our future aspirations. Our dream, yearning, and calling are to rebuild paradise. This impacts everything we do today. Yes, the Jewish People have thirty-five hundred years of history that shapes our behavior, but all of this is to pull us to the future, on the path to paradise.

Jewish education, the body responsible for shaping Jewish identities, needs to enable its students to understand and act according to this pull of the future. All of Jewish education needs to culminate with action points of change. Maintaining the status quo is not the goal. We have a long and cherished past, but we do *not* want the future to look like the past. Question 2 invites our students to imagine how their futures could be different, based on how they have understood and personalized their learning.

> Rav Kook writes that unlike all other cultures, the Jewish People is not a product of its past but of its future.

I don't think our students go home and wonder how their learning will fit into and affect their lives. The personalizing part of our educational process has to be a formal and essential part of the learning structure. But it is still not enough.

Engaging Through Sharing

Step 4, heartful engagement, actually has two parts: (1) personally processing in writing, which we just covered, and (2) sharing with a partner. Steps 3 and 4, mindful and heartful engagement, can be summarized in a three-part formula: "Learn—Process—Share."

To fully bring the learning into our hearts, we need talk about what we have written. We need to have a heart-to-heart conversation. We human beings are unique because of our ability to talk, and what we have been processing and writing about doesn't become completely real for us until we talk about it with others.

After participants have written their answers to the four questions, I invite them to take a partner and to share in private what they wrote. I emphasize that there is no pressure to share. Everyone should share only what they feel comfortable sharing, and it is also perfectly fine to pass.

In the partner conversation, one person talks for three to five minutes, and then the partners switch. This component of Soulful Education is extremely private and enables the students to overcome their inhibitions, to speak openly and truthfully.

The goal is to create a quality conversation focused on how the students have imagined that their learning could potentially affect their lives. At Ayeka, we call this exercise a spiritual *chevruta* (partnership), and it is one of the distinguishing aspects of Soulful Education. We sought to create a method that allows us to personalize and actualize the wisdom of Jewish sources and offers us the opportunity for personal growth.

This is done through active, nonjudgmental listening. Spiritual *chevruta* partners create safe space where they can talk openly without any concern of being criticized, attacked, or disregarded. A spiritual *chevruta* welcomes the sharing of an inner life without pressure or expectations. Partners can choose to open up a little or a lot, as they deem appropriate. There is no anxiety over what will happen if one chooses to explore new territory with the other person, since trust has been established. Spiritual *chevruta* partners are able to elicit for each other what was previously guarded. They are souls evoking one another.

This connection is characterized by confidentiality, trust, and caring. A great responsibility devolves upon the spiritual *chevruta* partner as he or she temporarily becomes the most important person in the partner's life.

We have found the following guidelines helpful for creating a mutually beneficial spiritual *chevruta* experience:

Spiritual *chevruta* partners:

- Guard the confidentiality of whatever is said.
- Create a safe space for the other to listen to his or her inner voice.
- Set aside everything in his or her own life and endeavor to be fully present for the other.
- Respect the uniqueness and worth of the other's journey.
- Are not curious for his or her own sake; he or she is careful not to invade the other's private space.
- Listen attentively, without judgment, cynicism, or joking.
- Ask open, reflective questions.
- Do not give advice or guide the other toward a certain answer.

Spiritual *chevruta* partners do not switch the focus back to themselves by saying things like:

- "I know just how you feel."
- "The same thing happened to me."
- "That's just what I would have done."

While these comments express identification with your partner, they also shift the focus from your partner to yourself. This is your time to give a precious gift to your partner: your undivided listening.

Quality listening is the key element here. We stress that one of the greatest acts of kindness people can do for each other is to listen fully. The difference between listening 100 percent and 80 percent is not 20 percent. It is an entirely different experience. Very few people can actually listen 100 percent without hesitation or judgment.

I noticed several years ago that when I am in the presence of three particular people, I suddenly become more confident, profound, and articulate. I love that feeling, but it only happens when I am in the presence of these three friends. I wondered, is it that only these three people encourage "the better me"? It quickly became clear to me that they are actually the only people in my life who listen to me 100 percent. They had cleared out a place in their lives to just be there with me, and consequently I deeply listened to myself.

Nelle Morton, an early feminist thinker, coined the phrase "Hearing each other to speech." We usually think that when two people are having a conversation, the person talking is the active one and the person listening is the passive one. Nelle Morton's observation actually flips this perception on its head. It is the person listening who is active and begins the process. Only when the listener is fully present and focused can the speaker then begin to access and discover his or her true story. The listener "hears"—leads—the other person *to* his or her personal story. This is what happened to me with my three friends. When someone listens deeply to me, I begin to listen deeply to myself.

In our busy, multi-tasking world, quality conversations have become extremely uncommon. Rarely do we have the opportunity for someone to listen to us 100 percent. This is the goal of the spiritual *chevruta*. Even though the *chevruta* conversation is not long, it can be intimate, powerful, authentic, and bonding.

Tragically, the most important conversations of our lives are the ones we may never have. Judaism provides endless possibilities for these conversations, yet rarely, if ever, will we use our sources to prompt these conversations in the classroom. No one will ever directly ask:

- "How are you doing with your gratitude, and how would your life be different if you were more grateful?"
- "How is your relationship with God? What would be different about your life if you had a closer relationship?"
- "How is your relationship with your parents? What small step do you think you could take to make it better?"
- "How are you doing with your jealousy? What would be different about you if all of a sudden you let go of some of your jealous tendencies?"
- "How is your connection with people who think differently than you? What is a small step you could take to become a more tolerant person?"

Most of us are too shy to enter into these challenging conversations. But the guidelines of heartful engagement actually make it much safer to pose such difficult questions. For the speakers, the talking is easy, because they know they will not be judged, they will be listened to 100 percent, and the conversation will be held in confidence. For the listeners, the listening is easy, because there is no pressure to say something insightful, ask a deep question, or offer sage advice.

> If we want to create worlds for our students, we need to contract ourselves and make space for them.

The "no giving advice" rule is the essential prerequisite for honestly opening up and talking. The speaker knows that he or she will not be evaluated for his or her honesty. There is no need to become defensive, because their words won't be judged or rated. This is not an exercise to fix each other; the answers need to come from within, from listening to the voice of the soul.

When we started these conversations several years ago, I had a hunch that they would prove to be personally meaningful and enriching. I've been greatly surprised, though, at how bonded participants often become through their brief sharing. Countless times I have witnessed new friendships form and old friendships deepen through this spiritual *chevruta*.

This moment of spiritual *chevruta* is, in fact, the climax and highlight of the class. It is our main course. Often I have heard, "I thought I knew this person really well, but we had never spoken about this subject." A married couple shared that their spiritual *chevruta* enabled the best conversation they have had in years.

The *Tzimtzum* of Teaching

For me, the teacher, the time of spiritual *chevruta* is extremely challenging and frustrating. I love when my students talk in class; I know what is happening and am able to control the intellectual airspace of my classroom. But I will never know what students say to each other during their spiritual *chevruta* time.

The Kabbalah relates that God created this world through *tzimtzum*, a self-contraction to make space for us. This is the model for us as educators: if we want to create worlds for our students, we need to contract ourselves and make space for them. I am dying to know what the students are sharing with each other, but I will never know.

> In Soulful Education, the class can become the springboard for soulful conversations that build and deepen trust and friendship.

I can tell that they are having a quality conversation by observing their gesturing and the focus in their eyes. The most important moment of my teaching will remain a mystery and hidden from me. A different kind of bond is created between teacher and students during the time of spiritual *chevruta*. The students sense that I trust them to handle their own space. They realize that I am honoring them by removing myself from the center and ceding my need to control the class. I am acknowledging that they have their own unique inner voices. Even though I am on the sidelines, the fact that I have opened up the space for them, allowing them to discover their own words without intervention, deepens the bonds of trust between us immeasurably. It is my greatest way of honoring them.

There is a beautiful expression in Hebrew: "Words that come out of one person's heart enter into the heart of another." In Soulful Education, the class can become the springboard for soulful conversations that build and deepen trust and friendship.

Step 5

Summarizing the Learning

What is your take-away from today?

We have already done so much. We have:

- Transitioned into the learning space.
- Framed the learning in a personal way.
- Learned with an open mind.
- Processed and personalized the learning through writing and sharing.

Aren't we done?

Not yet. There are two more steps in a full Soulful Education paradigm. To continue our meal metaphor, it's time to move on to dessert. Like dessert, step 5 is very sweet. It closes the meal. Before the students walk out of class, they need to crystallize their own personal take-away from our session.

I cannot count the number of times I have had this conversation with people as they come out of a class:

"How was class?"
"Great. Great class."
"Share a bit. What was it about?"
"Oh, you had to be there."
"What did you get out of it?"
"So much."
"Give me one thing."
"Oh, you had to be there."

79

I am suspect of answers like "Oh, you had to be there." In other words, the person is saying, "I really don't have a handle on it. It's kind of all swirling around. I can't articulate anything in particular because it's pretty unclear and fading away." Even the best classes have a tendency to become blurry and disappear quickly.

This situation can be frustrating for both the student and the teacher. One moment, everyone was into it. The next, it's as if we've all been hit with amnesia. So many times I have begun a class by asking, "What did we talk about last time?" only to encounter blank faces staring back at me.

Step 5 is creating a personal summary. The students are asked to respond to a simple question: "What are you taking away from today's session?"

Students can record their answers however they like: in bullet form, as poetry, or as free-flowing prose. They may note just one point or as many as they want. Sometimes I ask a few students to volunteer to share with the group, and sometimes I just let them write in silence without sharing.

The whole process takes only a couple of minutes, but it enables the students to reflect, crystallize, and concretize for themselves what was significant for them in the class. It offers them closure, and they leave with a sense of satisfaction that they actually did get something out of our time together.

Step 6

Transitioning Out of the Class

The goal of the class is what happens after the class is over.

Since the most important educational moment for the student happens after the class is over, our educational GPS must be set for "life after the class." The most important piece of our teaching is setting this piece into place. How can we get our students to bring the learning into their lives?

For so many years, I completely ignored this aspect of education. I was so happy that a class was successful that I immediately began to focus on the next class. I spent so much time preparing myself for the class itself; I didn't spend *any* time preparing the students for life after the class.

Maimonides states that escorting guests out of one's home is actually a greater mitzvah than welcoming them into one's home.[9] When I welcome guests into my home, I am thinking about the wonderful conversations we will have and how we will enjoy each other's company. But hours later, when the meal is over and the conversations have finished, what am I thinking? Usually about how much I have to clean up and then how to get ready for tomorrow and get on with my life. The guests have already served their purpose in providing a very pleasurable evening. They don't have anything more to offer me.

This is why Jewish law stresses the importance of escorting the guests out and helping them on their way. This is a purely giving act, focused on the continued and future well-being of the guests. "Someone who does not escort guests out—it is as if he has shed their blood."[10] If after the meal I am solely focused on getting on with my own life, it is as if I have neglected my guests' well-being and future safety. Despite my exhaustion and need to prepare for tomorrow, I have to escort my guests on their way.

Teaching is no different. Even after I have taught a class, when I am totally exhausted and already feeling pressure to prepare for the next, I stop and escort the students out of the class and into their lives. I am not physically escorting them, but ensuring that their way out will be enriched by their experience in our classroom.

Soulful Education has discovered two essential elements for bringing the learning into life:

- The seed for "after the class" must be sowed during the class.
- Each student must have a partner.

Where do we plant this seed? During the writing exercise. The fourth and last question was:

- If you could give yourself one small but practical piece of advice to help you grow, based on what we have learned together, what piece of advice would you give yourself?

The key word in this question is "small." We are encouraging small steps, not dramatic life overhauls. Change and personal growth are extremely difficult. Trying to take a *big* step sets us up for a *big* fall and letdown. The post-class goal is for the students to allow their new learning to impact their lives in very small, measured steps.

Follow-up is now easy. Each student takes a partner—it could be the partner of their spiritual *chevruta*—and the partners check in with one another during the week. All they need to ask is, "How are you doing with that piece of advice you gave yourself?" Nothing complicated—the two students can simply text-message each other a couple of times during the week.

The post-class communication achieves a few valuable educational goals:

- It brings the learning into the lives of the students.
- It further bonds the students with the subject matter and with each other.
- It keeps the class topics alive, so that when the class meets again the students don't have to struggle to remember what we talked about.

Why do the students need partners? Why can't they just take their own advice and apply it to their lives? Because it is simply too difficult to change ourselves by ourselves. We are too attached to our comfort zones and the status quo. I would like to work on parts of myself, but my habits are so entrenched in my psyche that I am virtually helpless to address them by myself. Self-help groups are built on this wisdom, acknowledging that we need external support, even to take the smallest step toward change.

The partner who is encouraging me to take the advice that I offered myself—in writing—is not a mentor, therapist, or expert. She or he is a friend who is offering a listening ear, encouragement, and support. Often that is all I need.

It is simply too difficult to change ourselves by ourselves.

I've worked with teachers who have been more creative and proactive in this follow-up. They have set up email lists and closed Facebook pages that the students use to comment on how they are bringing the learning into their lives.

To my surprise, the great majority of students enjoy this process. Overwhelmingly, they comment on how they enjoy hearing about their classmates' progress and how much the follow-up deepens their friendships.

Conclusion

I tried to say it boldly. I tried to shout it from the rooftop.

It is time for Jewish education to focus on the future. It's all about "becoming."

There's a lot of panic in today's Jewish world. People are frantically worried about the drop-off rate of this generation. Not only the young are disconnecting. Jews of all ages are feeling their Jewish identity withering. The passion is fading. "Been there, done that" is how we feel about our Judaism.

This panic leads our rabbis, educators, and leaders to grasp at quick fixes and gimmicks, trying to entice the young and engage the not-so-young. Innovation, more innovation, and more cutting-edge, glitzy, techno-hip tricks. It is not a surprise that these desperate measures don't seem to work.

> It is time for Jewish education to focus on the future. It's all about "becoming."

Soulful Education wants us to calm down, to pause and remember that Judaism is serious. It is profound. It is relevant and meaningful. It is still the best vehicle for personal, spiritual, communal, and national growth. We need to understand that first and foremost, Judaism is about the possibility of change and hope in the world, not tribal continuity and cultural connection.

- Abraham argued with God, relentlessly asking, "What if …?" (Genesis 18).

- Moses freed a nation of slaves from masters whom no one had ever escaped.
- Countless prophets refused to accept a dismal status quo.

We are all about the future. We are constantly being called to the future. Our vision and mission are to make this world reflect the image of God, to rebuild the Garden of Eden. We are not just about doing, and we are not just about being; we are about becoming.

Soulful Education invites each of us to continually take our small steps in that direction, to become our better and even better selves. Our repository of wisdom is the fuel tank for our growth. When we fill ourselves up with the wisdom of thirty-five hundred years, we have the power, energy, vision, and desire to continue on our journey. When we establish safe space for learning, with love and support for each other, then we are not afraid to risk moving out of our comfort zones, to enable one another to take small steps of change.

> Soulful Education invites each of us to continually take our small steps in that direction, to become our better and even better selves.

Rav Kook called us to educate with our imagination. We need to envision a people collectively moving toward paradise, one step at a time.

I need to remember that I am a product of my future. I am not lost and I am not stuck. Jewish wisdom and the voice of my soul dare me to live my authentic life.

Appendix

Ayeka-cizing Classes

Parker J. Palmer writes:

> I have heard that in the training of therapists, which involves much
> practical technique, there is this saying: "Technique is what you use
> until the therapist arrives." Good methods can help a therapist find
> a way into the client's dilemma, but good therapy does not begin
> until the real-life therapist joins with the real life of the client.
> Technique is what teachers use until the real teacher arrives.[1]

The "real life" that Palmer is referring to is the full inner life of the therapist, or in our case, of the teacher.

"Good teaching cannot be reduced to technique; good teaching comes
from the identity and integrity of the teacher."[2]

The essence of this book is to convey an educational approach rooted
deeply in identity and integrity—a seemingly small shift that naturally
becomes part of a teacher's "real-life," day-to-day educational approach,
and thereby changes everything. The aim is for educators to internalize
these principles, to integrate them deeply into every aspect of their teaching. Hopefully, this isn't rocket science; once introduced to this "com-
monsense"—but seldom actualized—approach, teachers will implement
it intuitively and thereby "automatically" enhance the engagement and
impact made in their classrooms. As their experience with these techniques
grows, soulful educators continue to refine the balance, finding that they
simply "know" when to share personal stories, "feel" when students have
slipped back into "disengaged intellect" mode and need to process and

personalize, "sense" when "safe space" is in danger of violation, and "intuit" when students need help to transition back from multi-tasking. The soulful educator's personal grappling with these issues will further sensitize him or her to the experience of the students, resulting in a teacher who is not just presenting material, but "totally there" in the classroom, with his or her personal identity and integrity fully engaged.

As part of the ongoing journey for becoming a soulful educator, Ayeka recommends work on both levels that Palmer has described: "real life" and "technique."

"Technique" includes the pedagogic skills, tools, and teaching aids that teachers employ as their tricks of the trade. They do not flow naturally from a teacher's "inner being," but rather are external to them. When teachers start "techniquing," students sense it immediately—an awareness that they are remembering or quoting something that isn't really part of them—something that, in Palmer's words, has not become part of the teacher's identity and integrity. *Nonetheless, technique is important as an enabler.* By practicing technique, the teacher improves control over the classroom, resulting in an increased ease and confidence that make room for the emergence of an engaged "real-life" approach. To this end, techniques are important facilitators for Soulful Education.

So this appendix will focus on technique.

We thought it would be helpful to offer a number of "how-to" examples—concrete demonstrations of how any subject can be "Ayeka-cized." The goal is to illustrate that every subject in Jewish learning, every *sugya* (Talmudic passage) and every chapter, has the potential to speak directly and personally to us and to our students.

In the following pages, we offer example introductions to a variety of subject and writing exercises, each of which serves as an invitation to students to personalize their learning. As mentioned earlier in the chapter "What Does It Mean to Be a Soulful Teacher?," teachers should not be "framing" the subject in each and every classroom session. However, when weeks or months will be devoted to teaching a single topic, it is important to frame and reframe the learning with beginnings, ends, and progress markers that connect and reconnect the students—as well as the teacher!—to the material in a personal, life-impacting way.

Ideally, a blending of Parker J. Palmer's two levels will occur. The "real-life" and "technique" levels will merge. The vision of Soulful Education is that gradually, for both teachers and students, the techniques of Soulful Education will help bring the subjects studied into their real lives.

Ayeka-cizing a Class on *Chumash*

Theme: Jealousy
Sources: Genesis 4:1–8; Ramban, commentary on Genesis 4:7

Genesis 4:1–8

1. And the man knew Eve his wife; and she conceived and bore Cain, and said: "I have acquired a man with the help of God."
2. She gave birth again, to his brother, Abel. Abel was a keeper of sheep, but Cain was a tiller of the ground.
3. At the end of the season Cain brought, of the fruits of the ground, an offering to God.
4. And Abel also brought an offering of the firstlings of his flock and the best parts thereof. And God turned in favor to Abel and to his offering.
5. But to Cain and to his offering He did not turn favorably. And Cain was very distressed, and his face fell.
6. And God said to Cain: "Why are you distressed? Why has your face fallen?
7. "If you do your best, you will be able to lift up your face. And if you do not do your best—sin crouches at your door; and it desires you, but you may rule over it."
8. And Cain spoke to Abel his brother....
9. And it came to pass, when they were in the field, that Cain rose up against Abel his brother, and slew him.

Ramban, Commentary on Genesis 4:7

Why did Cain's face fall? His face fell because he was embarrassed over the success of his brother, and in his jealousy he killed him.

Introducing the Subject to the Class

The account of Cain and Abel is the first story in the Torah outside of the Garden of Eden. This is the Torah's first statement of life in "the real world." It is a painfully tragic story of disappointment, aggression, and fratricide. There are many points to be discussed in this section: Cain's naming, the bringing of sacrifices, the difference in the sacrifices, God's response to Cain and Abel, the poetic and challenging language of verse 7, the missing conversation of verse 8, and Cain's response to the rejection of his sacrifice.

Amid these points, the issue of jealousy has to emerge. As the Ramban points out, Cain's disappointment stemmed more from the acceptance of his brother's sacrifice than from the rejection of his own.

To this end, I would introduce the class like this:

> I would like to believe that I am not a jealous person. I would like to believe that I have worked through the petty feelings of jealousy and am a fully confident and self-secure human being. I really would like to believe that. But it is not completely true, and it may never be. In fact, I probably experience pangs of jealousy some time every day.
>
> All you have to say to me is: "Dear Teacher, I just went to this other class and—wow—it is the best class I ever took!"
>
> My instinctive reaction? Not being overjoyed that you found a class that you're excited about and works for you, but rather a voice clicks inside of me and snarls, "What about my class? What's wrong with me?"
>
> I admit that this is a very small way of responding. I am definitely not proud of it. But it's there.
>
> Jealousy. It is probably the most basic human response to the world. I would say that it's how God hard-wired us. That's our story—Cain and Abel. Two people in the world and we have to deal with jealousy.
>
> And it starts at the youngest age. Try this simple experiment: On a hot summer day, ask two little kids if they would like some ice cream. Then give each of them an incredible ice cream cone with sprinkles, chocolate syrup, and nuts. And then, put a cherry on just *one* of them. Hand the cones to the kids and watch what happens. I'll bet anything that the

kid without the cherry will throw a major tantrum. "Why did he get a cherry? Where's my cherry? I want one too! Waah."

Will the kid be happy getting the gift of the "almost perfect" ice cream cone with sprinkles, chocolate, and nuts? Or will he go ballistic because the other kid got a cherry and he felt left out? My bet is on the cherry disaster. Why is that?

Because jealousy is the most natural feeling in the world. It's the Torah's way of saying: Welcome to the real world.

And it doesn't go away. The tendency to compare does not simply go away. We need to recognize this tendency and work to overcome it; otherwise, there is a strong possibility that we will spend our entire lives comparing ourselves to others—with plenty of damaging fallout.

I've spent a lot of time asking people what they tend to compare about themselves to others, and I see that their answers fit into patterns:

- In their teen years, people compare their academic, athletic, and creative achievements.
- In their twenties, people compare career and other personal accomplishments.
- In their thirties and forties, people compare families, children, and financial status.
- In their fifties, people compare their midlife crises.
- In their sixties and seventies, people compare the achievements of their children and grandchildren, and so on.

It doesn't go away, but we can become more aware of it. We don't have to let it control us. We may have a Cain-voice within us, but we don't have to let it rule over us.

I'm excited to study this story again. As the story continues, jealousy can lead to aggression—and it never leads to happiness. I may still have that Cain-voice within me, urging me to compare and find my self-worth by thinking that I am better than someone else. It may never disappear entirely. Nevertheless, I can work to control and overcome it. I really hope that through our learning together I will discover new insights and the willpower to rule over this voice of jealousy.

I know—in my head—that everything about me is singularly me, that I am unique. God created me in a way that almost defies comparison. I have a unique face, unique voice, unique fingerprints, and unique taste buds. Everything about me is different and unique. Yet I still struggle and am a work-in-progress regarding jealousy.

Every story in the Torah conveys an eternal message. For me, this is one of the most powerful and personally relevant ones.

End of my introduction. I would then ask if any of the students could identify with my personal quandary and hear from them if they have ever felt confused or conflicted about this issue. Then we would study the sources, most likely including the ones noted above and others. I would remind the students that although they may have known each other for a long time and be very close friends, this may be a subject they have not spoken about personally with each other.

It is a subject that evokes our insecurities and vulnerability. Jealousy is a quality that none of us is immune from.

We need to create a safe space in which everyone feels honored and safe. No one should feel judged or invalidated. No one has the right to shut someone else down.

After the Class Discussion

After we have learned the sources and examined the ideas in class, I would invite the students to write, in silence, their responses to the following questions:

- On the "jealousy meter" of 1 to 10, with 1 being "I never get jealous" and 10 being "I am always jealous," what number would you give yourself? Where are you vis-à-vis the quality of jealousy? After you give yourself a number, write a few sentences about why you chose that number in particular.

- If you could magically become less jealous, if you could drop down a few numbers on the jealousy meter, what would be different in your life?
- What do you think is holding you back from becoming less jealous? What are the specific obstacles that you need to work on?
- What piece of very practical advice would you give to yourself to help you take a small step in becoming less jealous?

After they have had the opportunity to write, it is time for spiritual *chevruta*. I would ask them to partner with another student and share whatever they feel comfortable with regarding their answers. Each one talks for four or five minutes, and then they switch.

After the Class

During the classes we will have learned the sources, reflected on and personally processed the learning, and then shared with another student. But the goal of the class is not the class, but the lives of our students. After the class is over, the students would then be instructed to check in with their spiritual *chevruta* partners (in person or through messaging) several times during the upcoming week, asking, "How are you doing with the piece of advice you wanted to give to yourself? Where are you now on the jealousy meter?"

Hopefully, our learning and personal processing will bring us to a deeper connection to this story in the Torah as we will have taken a step to becoming a better version of ourselves.

Ayeka-cizing a Class on Talmud

Theme: The stubborn and rebellious child
Source: Talmud, *Sanhedrin* 68b–72a

Talmud, *Sanhedrin* 68b–72a

Mishnah (68b): A stubborn and rebellious child: when does he become liable to the penalty of a stubborn and rebellious child?... Gemara (72a): It has been taught: Rabbi Yossi HaGalili said: Did the Torah decree that the rebellious child will be brought before the courts and stoned merely because he ate a pound of meat and drank a bottle of Italian wine? But the Torah foresaw his eventual destiny. For at the end, after dissipating his father's wealth, he would still seek to satisfy his accustomed gluttony, and being unable to do so, he would attack people on the roads and rob them. Therefore the Torah said, "Let him die while still innocent, and let him not die guilty."

Introducing the Subject to the Class

Talmud can be taught on many levels:

- Beginning: this level focuses primarily on the acquisition of skills, how to understand the Talmud's Aramaic, and how to punctuate and follow the basic flow of the page.
- Intermediate: how to understand the logic and reasons involved in the Talmudic discussions.
- Advanced: how to read and decipher the Talmudic commentaries—from Rashi and *Tosafot* to the *Rishonim*.
- Scholarly: how to understand the concepts underlying each opinion and see the patterns of thought emerging in the larger Talmudic context.

In addition to learning the specific content of the tractate, the process of learning Talmud connects students with the world of the Rabbis, the tradition of Jewish thought, and the foundations of Jewish practice. Studying Talmud can be an intellectual, historical, and even mystical experience, transporting the students into another time and world while engaging in ageless conversations seeking truth and holiness.

Soulful Education adds another level to this experience. Our questions, as soulful educators, are "How can our students *personally* connect to what they are learning? How can this experience of learning Talmud affect the behavior of our students—*after* the class is over?" In addition to teaching Talmud on any of the levels mentioned above, we think about how to make the *sugyot* (content) personally meaningful and relevant. For many—in fact, maybe even for most—sections of the Gemara, this can be a challenging task.

This section of the Talmud (*Sanhedrin* 68b–72a) presents an idea that can easily be dismissed as unrealistic and irrelevant by the students. In fact, the Talmud itself declares, "There has never been a 'stubborn and rebellious child,' and there never will be! Why then was the law written? So that you can study it and receive reward" (*Sanhedrin* 71a).

If the "stubborn and rebellious child" never existed, how can we possibly demonstrate its eternal wisdom and relevance?

To foster a deeper connection, I would introduce the class like this:

> The Gemara states that the "stubborn and rebellious child" does not exist. Never has and never will. It does not matter how egregious his or her behavior may currently be, Judaism will never execute a child because of what he or she might do in the future.
>
> Yet, the seed of the "stubborn and rebellious child" really does exist—within each of us.
>
> And though no one would call me a child, I still have a "stubborn and rebellious child" voice within me. It urges me to be selfish, thoughtless, gluttonous, rude, arrogant, and entitled. It tells me to disregard the advice of others, to disrespect the words of my elders, and to neglect and disdain my peers.
>
> I can state with confidence today that though this "stubborn and rebellious child" talks to me, it does not control or define me. But, once, it started to.
>
> I played a lot of sports in my youth, especially baseball and football in high school. In college I worked out and jogged. I regarded myself as an athlete. Years went by and I still maintained this image of myself. I continued to keep in decent shape and had a pretty healthy diet.
>
> I had one habit that I knew wasn't so great for me, but I also thought that it was not such a big deal. I justified it by saying to myself, "Everyone has some guilty pleasure, and this one is really not so terrible." What did I do? Before going to sleep I loved to eat two bologna sandwiches. Sometimes

more than two. Sometimes a lot more. People who knew about this, my family, friends, and even a doctor or two, told me that it wasn't good for me. But I didn't care what they thought and didn't listen to them. I said to myself that I knew better and it was not a big deal.

Years went by. Now I'm not exercising so much, but still I picture myself as an athlete. And I continue to eat my bologna sandwiches late at night before going to sleep.

Sometimes I would get on the scale and be shocked at what it said, but then I would go into denial and say to myself that the scale must have been off. I couldn't possibly weigh that much!

Needless to say, over a fifteen-year period, those bologna sandwiches started to add up. Now I was twenty pounds overweight, huffing and puffing up steps, and with a cholesterol problem. My doctor read me the riot act: I had to stop eating my beloved bologna sandwiches. Finally, I woke up.

Dropping those twenty pounds was a huge challenge and took a long time. Now, looking back, I am astonished at how oblivious I was to the process of gaining them. I am blown away by how stuck I had gotten in a bad habit, how I had deluded myself into seeing myself as the athlete of my youth, and how I didn't notice what it had done to me.

This experience provoked a lot of self-reflection. What other small or unimportant habits might I be developing? What other small things could move me in a direction I don't really want to go?

This Gemara is giving us an important insight into ourselves: we may be doing seemingly minor and insignificant acts that eventually may become destructive, to ourselves and others.

The idea of seeing our behaviors in a future context is an important one. The "stubborn and rebellious child" was judged by where he would ultimately end up, "his eventual destiny."

Our Gemara is inviting us to ask ourselves, "What are the relatively small things that I am doing or not doing in my life that could build a momentum that could end up somewhere quite negative? Are there things in my own behavior that I am dismissing because they are 'not a big deal' simply because I would rather avoid them? Is there a small problem in my life that could grow into a big one if I am not careful?"

I'm excited and looking forward to studying these pages of Gemara with you. Even though I may have dealt with my bologna sandwich issue, I know that I am still a work-in-progress in many other things. I'm looking forward to being provoked and challenged by this Gemara to examine where else in my life resides the "stubborn and rebellious child." Its voice never completely disappears. I really hope that by the end of learning this section with you, I'll be able to take a small step in my life to better eradicate, or at least control, this voice within me.

End of my introduction. I would then ask if any of the students could identify with this issue and my personal situation.

Then we would study the pages of this *sugya*. Most likely, it would take several weeks. I would remind the students that although they may have known each other for a long time and be very close friends, this may be a subject they have not spoken about personally with each other.

It is a subject that evokes our insecurities and vulnerability. Jealousy is a quality that none of us is immune from.

We need to create a safe space in which everyone feels honored and safe. No one should feel judged or invalidated. No one has the right to shut someone else down.

After the Class Discussion

After we have learned the sources and examined the ideas in class, I would invite the students to write, in silence, their responses to the following questions:

- Where in my life do I identify the seeds of a "stubborn and rebellious child"? Are there issues in my life that I have ignored or discounted because they are small? Is it possible they could grow into something larger?

- How would my life be different if I could change these small acts and behavior patterns?
- What is holding me back from changing them? What obstacles do I need to overcome?
- What small piece of advice would I give to myself to help me counteract this voice of the "stubborn and rebellious child"?

After they have had the opportunity to write, it is time for spiritual *chevruta*. I would ask them to partner with another student and share whatever they feel comfortable with regarding their answers. Each one talks for four or five minutes, and then they switch.

After the Class

During the classes we will have learned the sources, reflected on and personally processed the learning, and then shared with another student. But in Soulful Education, the goal of the class is what happens after the class is over. We want to bring Jewish knowledge not only into their minds, but also into their lives. After the class is over, the students would then be instructed to check in with their spiritual *chevruta* partners (in person or through messaging) several times during the upcoming week, asking, "How are you doing with the piece of advice you wanted to give to yourself?"

Hopefully, our learning and personal processing will bring us to a deeper connection to the wisdom of this *sugya* as we deal with the ever-present voice of the "stubborn and rebellious child" within us.

Ayeka-cizing a Class of *Tefilah*

Theme: Morning Blessings
Source: Prayer book

Prayer Book, Morning Blessings

Blessed are You, Lord our God, King of the universe, who opens the eyes of the blind.

Introducing the Subject to the Class

The Talmud refers to prayer as *avodah shebalev*—the service or work of the heart. This is because prayer—authentic, "heartfelt" prayer—comes straight from the heart.

But for the first ten years that I taught our prayer book's liturgy, I focused on everything but the heart. I focused on the history of the prayer's evolution, on the meaning of the words, on the context of the prayer within the overall structure of each prayer service. I believe this information is important—that it helps students deepen their understanding and appreciation for the wisdom and power of Jewish prayer. But I'm not sure how much it helped them develop into "prayerful" people.

Just as learning about art history does not develop artists and learning about literature does not develop writers, so learning *about* prayer does not necessarily develop hearts that turn toward God.

Part of the problem is due to the fundamental conundrum that underlies all "formalized" prayer: "How can any formulistic prayer—a collection of words put together by someone else—possibly be an authentic representation of my relationship with God? And even if a prayer represents how I feel today, given that my relationship with God is constantly changing, why should I repeat it—exactly the same words—day after day, decade after decade?"

It seems to me that these deeper issues—and many others on the same level—should be the real "content" that is addressed in *tefilah* class. Obviously it is important to give each prayer its due, to familiarize the students with the beauty and depth of the words, and to explore the place that the prayer has occupied in Jewish history. But the bottom line that we are aiming at—or at least that we ought to be aiming at—is to help our students become prayer-full human beings and to regard the siddur as useful for that pursuit.

Knowing the meaning of each prayer—becoming able to recite the words smoothly—is surely part of the process. But words that are not heartfelt fall empty. Part of our task as teachers—that is, hopefully, as prayer-full people ourselves—is to help the students develop their own relationship with God and to see the prayer book as a blueprint that moves the process forward.

As such, the importance of teaching prayer to the heart of the students is even greater than for other subjects. In virtually every other aspect of Judaism, even if our hearts are not connected to our behavior, our actions have meaning and can have a positive effect. The Rabbis concluded that mitzvot do not need *kavanah* (intention), as our actions, in and of themselves, reflect our consciousness. But in prayer, the only action we perform is the expression of our relationship with God. If we are not emotionally or spiritually connected with the words that come out of our mouths, the whole exercise is bereft of meaning. If there is no relationship between the thoughts in our head, the feelings in our hearts, and the words in our mouths, the exercise is incomplete.

Before the formal morning public service (*Shacharit*), we recite *Birchot HaShachar* (Morning Blessings), a string of fifteen blessings celebrating moments and actions in our individual physical lives—fifteen blessings, very similar in nature and language, recited consecutively. While centuries ago they were recited while actually performing the actions (i.e., when putting on clothes, one would say the blessing of getting dressed), they have now become a list of blessings declaimed independently of their corresponding actions. Recited every morning, this list can become a rote exercise devoid of personal connection. It is very easy to simply "knock them off" in a few breaths, without serious awareness, focus, or appreciation.

Our challenge is to foster a deeper connection with these blessings—to enable students to use them as a springboard for deeper awareness and thankfulness. To this end, I would introduce the class like this:

> I am really looking forward to studying these blessings together. Years ago, when I first discovered Judaism as an adult, I was really into these blessings. It was so meaningful for me that Judaism not only focused on spiritual or intellectual life, but also celebrated the body and physical life.
>
> Religions can often become disconnected from this world. I found it amazing that Judaism was so present in this world,

that it noticed and even sanctified the most everyday normal functions of living.

But then the routine of life began to diminish my enthusiasm. Saying the same prayers every day is very challenging, and I found it hard not to let them become rote.

In particular, *Birchot HaShachar* can seem like a laundry list. I found that I usually just mumbled them, "knocked them off," whether at home or at the beginning of the morning service. At *Shacharit*, they come at the very beginning of the service, and there is still so much to get through that I found it really hard to dwell on each blessing.

But a few years ago, life reminded me.

I was on a work trip, traveling around the country, staying at homes of friends. I had planned the whole trip around a Sunday seminar that I was to give to fifteen educators. The event had taken four months to plan.

I woke up Sunday morning, and out of the blue, my eyes didn't function. The room began spinning around and wouldn't stop. I couldn't stop the spinning to focus. I couldn't stand up, much less walk, without falling down and crashing.

I began to panic. I called out to my host and told him what was going on. He quickly Googled the symptoms (not a good idea) and said that I probably had a brain tumor. Aahh. Panic deepened.

He virtually carried me to the emergency room of the hospital. Turns out, it was a bout of vertigo. The doctors tilted my head in a few directions, and three hours later my eyesight returned to normal. I could stand and walk. When I asked them what brought this on, they replied that it was "idiopathic." There was no reason, no apparent cause. Things like this just happen once in a while.

Needless to say, we canceled the Sunday seminar.

The vertigo has never returned. It was just like that—idiopathic. Unknowable and unpredictable. And terribly frightening.

But it changed me. I had never fully considered that the simple act of opening and focusing my eyes was such a gift.

Ever since then, when I get up in the morning, I pause for several seconds before saying the blessing of thanking God for being able to open one's eyes. I know that for a brief time and for no reason at all, I lost my sight. I can't take it for granted now.

But, here's really the point I wanted to make: *Pokei'ach ivr'im*, "who opens the eyes of the blind," is only *one* of the fifteen blessings. There are fourteen others that I am not as mindful and aware of as I could be. *Birchot HaShachar* celebrates fifteen miracles that happen to us every day.

I really hope that by the end of our studying together I will have deepened my relationship not only with these blessings, but also with what they are marking. I want to become a more grateful human being. I want to appreciate every moment of my life. This morning routine is an opportunity to honor my relationship with God and my own body. I shouldn't just "knock off this list" of blessings. I have taken a step in my life to especially appreciate one of the blessings. But I'm still a work-in-progress regarding all of the others. I'm looking to take a small step in my life to live with greater focus and happiness. I hope that our learning together will be the springboard for achieving this change in my life.

End of my introduction. I would then ask if any of the students could identify with what I said and hear from them if they have a special relationship with any of these blessings. Then we would study more sources to deepen our understanding of the blessings. I would remind the students that we are in a "safe space" zone, without cynicism, judging, or attacking each other. Everyone needs to feel honored and safe, and no one should feel judged or invalidated. No one has the right to shut someone else down.

After the Class Discussion

After we have learned the sources and examined the ideas in class, I would invite the students to write, in silence, their responses to the following questions:

- On the "blessing meter" of 1 to 10, with 1 being "I just knock them off without really thinking about them" and 10 being "I fully focus on each blessing," what number would you give yourself? Where are you vis-à-vis these blessings? After you give yourself a number, write a few sentences about why you chose that number.
- If you could magically become more grateful and appreciative of the miracle of your physical being, what would be different in your life?
- What do you think is holding you back from having this awareness? What are the specific obstacles that you need to work on?
- What piece of very practical advice would you give to yourself to help you take a small step in becoming more aware and thankful for the gifts of your physical life?

After writing, it is time for spiritual *chevruta*. I would ask the students to partner and share whatever they feel comfortable with regarding their answers. Each one talks for four or five minutes, and then they switch.

After the Class

During the classes we will have learned more sources on these blessings, reflected on and personally processed the learning, and then shared with another student. But in Soulful Education, the goal of the class is what happens after the class is over. We want to bring Jewish knowledge not only into their minds, but also into their hearts and lives.

After the class is over, the students would then be instructed to check in with their spiritual *chevruta* partners (in person or through messaging) several times during the upcoming week, asking, "Did you pause and focus more on any particular blessing of *Birchot*

HaShachar? How did that affect your day? What gift are you most aware of today?"

Hopefully, our learning and personal processing will bring us all to a deeper connection to these blessings as we have taken a step to becoming a more grateful and better version of ourselves.

Ayeka-cizing a Class on Hanukkah

Theme: Miracles

Sources: Talmud, *Shabbat* 21b; prayer book, addition during Hanukkah to the *Amidah*; blessing over the lighting of the Hanukkah candles

Talmud, *Shabbat* 21b

> What is the reason for Hanukkah?
>
> Our tradition teaches: On the twenty-fifth of Kislev commence the days of Hanukkah, which are eight, on which lamentation for the dead and fasting are forbidden. For when the Greeks entered the Temple, they defiled all of the oils therein, and when the Hasmonean dynasty prevailed against them and defeated them, they searched and found only one jar of oil that had remained pure, which had been sealed by the High Priest. The jar contained sufficient oil for only one day's lighting, yet a miracle occurred and they were able to light the menorah for eight days.

Prayer Book, Addition During Hanukkah to the *Amidah* (Silent Standing Prayer)

> And for the miracles, and for the salvation, and for the mighty deeds, and for the victories, and for the wonders, and for the consolations, and for the battles which You performed for our forefathers in those days, at this time.

Blessing over the Lighting of the Hanukkah Candles

> Blessed are You, Lord our God, King of the universe, who has performed miracles for our forefathers, in those days at this time.

Introducing the Subject to the Class

The concept of miracles, one of the central themes of Hanukkah, can actually be a very personal and provocative subject. A class about Hanukkah can be an opportunity for the teacher and students to reflect on their own understanding about what miracles are and to explore their own personal relationships with the miraculous. The students may have already studied Jewish sources that deal with miracles—for example, you don't get more miraculous than the Exodus, the parting of the Red Sea, or receiving manna from heaven—but most likely, they haven't given the subject much thought, and especially not in terms of how miracles affect them personally.

As with the Ayeka approach to all subjects, what we are looking for isn't just to teach the students "about" miracles and miraculous moments in Jewish history, but for them—and us—to examine and reflect on what our learning about miracles can say to us, right now. It is an invitation for us to take a deep look at our understanding of the miraculous today and perhaps to see it working in our own lives.

To this end, I would introduce the Hanukkah class like this:

> I have always found the idea of miracles to be very compli-
> cated and even confusing. On the one hand, I grew up in a
> family that never talked about the existence of God, God's
> role in this world, and certainly not moments of divine
> intervention.
>
> I have a relative, my aunt Lisa, who is a world-class sci-
> entist. She was involved in the international DNA genome
> project and was considered to be "the authority on all
> things" in our family. Whenever she spoke at the dinner
> table, whatever she said on any subject, that was the end of
> the discussion. No one argued with Aunt Lisa.
>
> One time I mentioned that I thought that the creation of
> the world, and the creation of human beings in particular,
> was a miracle. She offered a dismissal shrug and replied,
> "It's all just random mutation. Every educated person knows

that. People who believe in miracles should return to the Middle Ages." End of conversation.

I felt quite embarrassed and even a drop ashamed that I could be so unsophisticated and medieval. My mind said to me, "Who am I to disagree with a world-renowned scientist? She is so much more knowledgeable than I am. She must be right." Whenever I talked about these things with her, I saw her eyes glaze over and felt foolish for my belief that God could actually intervene in this world.

On the other hand, I have experienced several mind-boggling coincidences in my life—events that I cannot attribute to random chance. I can't believe that they are anything but miraculous. These moments have been very real for me, even if I have a hard time explaining them to someone else, even if others think that I am primitive and unenlightened. In my heart, I believe in miracles.

My mind tells me one thing, and my heart tells me another. I'm a walking contradiction. As I said, this subject, for me, is very complicated and confusing, leaving me full of questions:

- Does a miracle actually happen, or does it just take place in the eyes of the beholder?
- Do events occur randomly, or is there a hidden divine hand that is orchestrating the world?
- Can two people see the same event and have completely different responses?
- Can miracles come in different sizes—some affecting multitudes of people in grand landscapes, with marvelous and earth-shattering phenomena that seem against the laws of nature; others that are quiet and personal, happening almost invisibly, as when a person is suddenly able to find the will and courage to change a long-standing habit?

At the time of Hanukkah, the Jewish People were living in the midst of the flourishing Greek culture. The Greeks were an exceedingly intellectual civilization, producing Socrates,

Plato, and Aristotle in three consecutive generations. From the same intellectual genus as my aunt Lisa, the Greeks considered the human mind to be our greatest gift. They would have considered belief in miracles to be inane.

Yet Hanukkah celebrates the occurrence of something in the time of the Greeks that was beyond our philosophic understanding. Something happened that transcended the laws of nature—a miracle. The story tells us that God exists and is still involved in this world. The Talmud relates that a small miracle happened in the midst of a physical and cultural war. For the Jewish People, like the Greeks, the mind is considered an esteemed and invaluable gift; however, there are events in this world that are impossible for the mind to understand, events that come from an invisible source, from the beyond.

And so I am excited that our class is going to focus on this subject of miracles. I want to have the opportunity to study these sources and focus on this issue together. I am tired of feeling confused about this subject. I would like to have more clarity and conviction. I would like for my mind and heart to be on the same wavelength. I'm hoping that through our studying together, I will be able to take a small step in working out the present contradiction that has been going on with me for a long time.

End of my introduction. I would then ask if any of the students could identify with my personal quandary and hear from them if they have ever felt confused or conflicted about this issue.

Then we would study the sources, most likely including the ones noted above and others. I would remind the students that although they may have known each other for a long time and be very close friends, this is probably a subject they have not spoken about personally with each other. They may be in very different places regarding God's intervention in this world and the role of miracles. We need to create a safe space in which everyone feels honored and able to express their true opinion, whether it sides with the absurdity or the omnipresence of miracles. No one should feel judged or invalidated. No one has the right to shut someone else down.

After the Class Discussion

After we have learned the sources and examined the ideas in class, I would invite the students to write, in silence, their responses to the following questions:

- Have you ever experienced a moment in your life that you would consider a miracle? Does this moment still affect you in some way?
- Would you like to become more open to seeing (or interpreting) moments and events in the world as miraculous?
- What do you think is holding you back from being more aware of miracles in your life?
- What piece of advice would you give to yourself that would help you see more miracles?

After they have had the opportunity to write, it is time for spiritual *chevruta*. I would ask them to partner with another student and share whatever they feel comfortable with regarding their answers. Each one talks for four or five minutes, and then they switch.

After the Class

During the classes we will have learned the sources, reflected and personally processed the learning, and then shared with another student. But the goal of the class is not the class, but rather our lives.

After having learned about Hanukkah, reflected on and personally processed the learning, and then shared with another student, the students would then be instructed to check in with their spiritual *chevruta* partners (in person or through messaging) several times during the upcoming week, asking, "How are you doing with the piece of advice you wanted to give to yourself?"

Hopefully, our learning and personal processing will bring us to a deeper connection to the eternal message of Hanukkah.

Ayeka-cizing a Class on *Halachah*

Theme: Making *Kiddush* in the place of a meal (*Kiddush b'makom se'udah*)

Sources: Talmud, *Pesachim* 100b–101a; *Shulchan Aruch, Orach Chayim* 273

Talmud, *Pesachim* 100b–101a

As for people who have sanctified the day [made *Kiddush*] in the synagogue:

Rav said: They have not fulfilled their obligation in respect of wine, but they have fulfilled their obligation in respect of *Kiddush*.

But Shmuel maintained: They have not fulfilled their obligation in respect to *Kiddush* either.

Then, according to Rav, why does he [the Reader] recite *Kiddush* at home? In order to acquit his children and his household [of their obligation].

And [according to] Shmuel, why must he recite *Kiddush* in the synagogue? In order to acquit travelers of their obligation, for they eat, drink, and sleep in the synagogue.

Now Shmuel is consistent with his view, for Shmuel said: *Kiddush* is [valid] only where the meal is eaten. From this it was understood that only [to move] from one house to another [is forbidden], but [to move] from one place to another in the same house is not [forbidden].

Said Rabbi Anan bar Tachlifa: On many occasions I was standing before Shmuel, when he descended from the roof to the ground and then recited [again] *Kiddush*.

Now Rabbi Huna too holds that *Kiddush* is [valid] only where the meal is eaten. For [on one occasion] Rabbbi Huna recited *Kiddush* and [then] his light was extinguished, whereupon he carried his utensils into the room of his son Rabba, where a candle was burning and recited *Kiddush* [again], and then ate something, which proves that he holds: *Kiddush* is [valid] only where the meal is eaten.

Now Rabba too holds: *Kiddush* is [valid] only where the meal is eaten. For Abaye said: When I was at the Master's [Rabba's] house, and he recited *Kiddush*, he would say to us: "Eat a little [here], lest by the time you reach your lodgings your candles may be extinguished, and if you do not recite *Kiddush* in the house where you eat you will not have fulfilled your obligation with the *Kiddush* of this place, because Kiddush is [valid] only where the meal is eaten."

Shulchan Aruch, Orach Chayim 273

1. *Kiddush* is valid only when it is made in the place of a meal....
2. If one made *Kiddush* in one setting in order to eat there and afterward changed his mind and decided to eat elsewhere, he must make *Kiddush* again in the place of his meal.
3. If one made *Kiddush* and did not partake in a meal, he has not fulfilled his obligation of *Kiddush*.

Introducing the Subject to the Class

There are several layers to a class on Jewish law (*halachah*). The most primary level is to introduce the legal responsibilities to the students. What behavior does *halachah* mandate?

On the next level, we want the students to understand the historical development that led to this conclusion, including the various opinions involved and the reasoning behind the decision. We want the students to appreciate the ideas, concepts, and philosophy underlying the law—both the letter and the spirit.

But the Soulful Education approach goes one step deeper in an attempt to bring the students a *personal connection* with the law, to be able to perform the actions with a deep intention—*kavanah*—that brings meaning to the behavior.

Fostering this connection can often be a challenging task in a *halachah* class, which often focuses on the dry, legal aspects of Jewish life, leaving many students distant. While a small group of students find intellectual stimulation in the law's intricate details, many more plod through the texts, unmoved and bored.

To foster deeper connection with the material, I would introduce this class like this:

> *Kiddush b'makom se'udah* seems to be a very important idea to the Rabbis: the expression is repeated five times in this short Gemara. But at first glance it didn't really seem that significant to me.
>
> If the goal is to sanctify (*m'kadesh*) Shabbat, then why is the meal—the eating of food—so important?
>
> Can it be—as it seems to say in the *halachah*—that if I say the words, the blessings, and drink wine to elevate the experience, but don't also eat a cracker or bread or a meal, then the words don't count? That I haven't fulfilled my obligation of *Kiddush*?
>
> Huh? The words of the *Kiddush* don't even mention food! *Kiddush* is all about time—specifically Shabbat—not about place (*makom*), and certainly not about food (*se'udah*)! In fact, doesn't it seem that food/place has nothing to do with time/Shabbat? Food and place are such "earthy" things, while Shabbat is an intellectual—even a spiritual—concept.
>
> If two people make the same *Kiddush* with exactly the same words and *kavanah*, but one follows it with a cracker or cake and the other doesn't, why should God care?
>
> I once had a friend who made the most spiritual *Kiddush*. We had little kids the same age, and we would often go to his family for Shabbat. He would close his eyes and sing the *Kiddush* in a soft, whispering voice, incredibly slowly. It took a really long time. For the kids, it seemed like forever. His kids, and mine too, were young, and they pretty much went berserk waiting for the food. A couple of years later the couple divorced. He went off to live in a community of meditators.
>
> Sometimes we can just get too spiritual.

It is important in Judaism to elevate and sanctify this world. Shabbat is a holy time. But Judaism does not want us to become so connected to the heavens that we lose our anchoring in this world. We need to be like Jacob's ladder, reaching the heavens and rooted in earth. The Talmud is telling us that our holiness needs to be connected to this world. We sanctify, make *Kiddush*, but attach ourselves to the physical, to place and food. *Ein Kiddush eleh b'makom se'udah*, "There is only *Kiddush* in a place of eating." Judaism may be unique among all religions in requiring that spirituality be connected to the physicality of this world.

I do not have a good singing voice, and I am not as spiritually connected as my friend was. But sometimes I know that I too can get carried away and become detached from this world. It happens sometimes when I am learning. I'll forget to call the kids or help my wife. It happens when I am so passionate about a project I am working on that I forget to eat.

Ein Kiddush eleh b'makom se'udah is an expression of balance of body and soul, of the physical and spiritual.

I am a work-in-progress regarding this balance. I, we, never get it perfectly. We need continual tweaking; sometimes we need to focus more on the spiritual and sometimes more on the physical.

Ein Kiddush eleh b'makom se'udah is an invitation to us all to reflect on how we find and maintain balance in our spiritual and physical lives.

End of my introduction. I would then ask if any of the students could identify with this issue and my personal quandary. I would hear from them if they have ever felt out of balance or the need to tweak the balance between body and soul.

Then we would study the sources, most likely including the ones noted above and others. I would remind the students that although they may have known each other for a long time and be very close friends, this may be a subject they have not spoken about personally with each other.

We need to create a safe space in which everyone feels honored and safe. We're not going to let anyone feel judged or invalidated. No one has the right to shut someone else down.

After the Class Discussion

After we have learned the sources and examined the ideas in class, I would invite the students to write, in silence, their responses to the following questions:

- If you were to express this idea of blending spirituality with physicality—*Ein Kiddush eleh b'makom se'udah*—in your own words, what would you write?
- If you were to write a *kavanah* for yourself, to say before saying *Kiddush*, to deepen your connection to Shabbat and *Kiddush*, what would you write?
- Have you ever struggled to harmonize the spiritual and physical in your life? How did you work that out?
- What piece of advice would you give to yourself to help you better balance the spiritual and physical in your life?

After they have had the opportunity to write, it is time for spiritual *chevruta*. I would ask them to partner with another student and share whatever they feel comfortable with regarding their answers. Each one talks for four or five minutes, and then they switch.

After the Class

During the classes we will have learned the sources, reflected on and personally processed the learning, and then shared with another student. But in Soulful Education, the goal of the class is what happens after the class is over. We want to bring Jewish knowledge not only into their minds, but also into their lives. After the class is over, the students would then be instructed to check in with their spiritual *chevruta* partners (in person or through messaging) several times during the upcoming week, asking, "How are you doing with the piece of advice you wanted to give to yourself? Did you have an especially physical or spiritual moment this week?"

Hopefully, our learning and personal processing will bring us to a deeper connection to this *halachah* and balancing the physical and the spiritual in our lives.

Notes

Introduction

1. William Deresiewicz, *Excellent Sheep: The Miseducation of the American Elite and the Way to a Meaningful Life* (New York: Free Press, 2014), 15.
2. Maharal, *Chiddushei Aggadot* 2:144.

Part 1: Laying the Foundation for Soulful Education

1. Abraham Isaac Kook, *Olat HaRaaya*, 1:11 (Jerusalem: Mossad HaRav Kook Publishing, 1978).
2. Shlomo Elyashiv, *Leshem Shebo V'Achlama*, 1:19 (Petrikov, CK: Mordecai Tchadarbaum Publishing, 1909).
3. Maimonides, *Mishneh Torah*, Laws of the Chosen House 4:1.
4. Isaac Luria, *Eitz Chayim* 2:2.
5. Kook, *Olat HaRaaya*, 1:11.
6. Rabbi Jonathan Sacks, former chief rabbi of Britain, teaches that God's name in the Torah, *Eheyeh asher Eheyeh* (Exodus 3:14), should be translated as "I will become that which I will become"; "The Dignity of Difference," *On Being*, www.onbeing.org/program/dignitydifference/188.
7. Parker J. Palmer, *To Know as We Are Known: Education as a Spiritual Journey* (San Francisco: HarperOne, 1993), 107.
8. Mark Nepo, *The Exquisite Risk: Daring to Live an Authentic Life* (New York: Harmony, 2006), 49.
9. Brené Brown, *Daring Greatly: How the Courage to Be Vulnerable Transforms the Way We Live, Love, Parent, and Lead* (New York: Avery, 2015), chap. 2.
10. Rainer Maria Rilke, *Letters to a Young Poet* (New York: Modern Library, 2001), 78.
11. Samson Raphael Hirsch, *Hirsch Commentary on the Torah* (Gateshead, UK: Judaica Press, 1982), "Leviticus," 527.
12. Maimonides, *Mishneh Torah*, Laws of Repentance 10:6.
13. Sefat Emet, *Parshat Vaetchanan* (Jerusalem, 1971), 20.
14. Abraham Isaac Kook, *Lights of Holiness*, 4:389, 390 (Jerusalem: Mossad HaRav Kook Publishing, 1990).
15. Abraham Isaac Kook, *Orot HaKodesh*, 4:2 (Jerusalem: Mossad HaRav Kook Publishing, 1990).

16. Sharon Daloz-Parks, *Big Questions, Worthy Dreams* (San Francisco: Jossey-Bass, 2000), chap. 1.
17. Kook, *Orot HaKodesh*, 4:389.

Part 2: The Six Essential Steps of Soulful Education

1. Rav Shagar, *Closing the Gate* (Efrat, Israel: Institute for the Advancement of Rav Shagar's Writings, 2011), chap. 1.
2. Ibid.
3. Abraham Isaac Kook, *Mussar Avicha*, 2:2 (Jerusalem: Mossad HaRav Kook Publishing, 1976).
4. Henri Nouwen, *Spiritual Direction: Wisdom for the Long Walk of Faith* (New York: HarperCollins, 2006), 92–93.
5. Abraham Isaac Kook, *Orot HaKodesh*, 3:247 (Jerusalem: Mossad HaRav Kook Publishing, 1984).
6. *Nefesh HaChayim*, chap. 14.
7. Abraham Isaac Kook, *Ein Aya, Berachot* (Jerusalem: Mossad HaRav Kook Publishing, 1987), 127.
8. *Exodus Rabbah* 29.
9. Maimonides, *Mishneh Torah*, Laws of Mourning, 14:2.
10. Ibid.

Appendix: Ayeka-cizing Classes

1. Parker J. Palmer, *The Courage to Teach* (San Francisco: Jossey-Bass, 2007), 6.
2. Ibid., 10.

About the Author

Aryeh Ben David is an educator, lecturer, and author. Aryeh grew up in the United States, moved to Israel in 1978, and taught at the Pardes Institute in Jerusalem from 1987 to 2007, including serving for several years as its director of spiritual education. Aryeh also served as the educational consultant for Hillel International from 2004 to 2007 and as the educational director of the Jerusalem campus of Livnot U'Lehibanot from 1993 to 1998.

Aryeh is the author of two previous books, *The Godfile: 10 Approaches to Personalizing Prayer* and *Around the Shabbat Table: A Guide to Fulfilling and Meaningful Shabbat Table Conversations*.

Aryeh founded Ayeka: Center for Soulful Jewish Education in 2007 (www.ayeka.org.il). Ayeka trains educators of all denominations, campus professionals, and staff of middle and high schools how to teach Jewish subjects with more soulfulness, personal meaning, and impact on life.

Ayeka has presently launched three tracks: Becoming a Soulful Educator, Becoming a Soulful Parent, and Becoming a Soulful Rabbi. Future tracks include Becoming a Soulful Individual and Becoming a Soulful Professional. The vision of Ayeka is to help us take steps to Become a Soulful Society.

Aryeh received rabbinical ordination from the Israeli Rabbinate, served in the Israeli army, and lives with his wife Sandra and their six children and grandchildren in Israel.

CPSIA information can be obtained
at www.ICGtesting.com
Printed in the USA
LVHW032139230421
685340LV00018B/225